D1054830

The *Good News* of the *Holy Spirit*

Acts

Kevin Perrotta
Gerald Darring

**Six Weeks
with the Bible
for Catholic Teens**

6

Exploring
God's Word

LOYOLAPRESS.
CHICAGO

LOYOLAPRESS.

3441 N. ASHLAND AVENUE
CHICAGO, ILLINOIS 60657
(800) 621-1008
WWW.LOYOLABOOKS.ORG

Copyright © original text Kevin Perrotta. First published in 2001 as *Acts: The Good News of the Holy Spirit*, part of the series *Six Weeks with the Bible*, by Loyola Press, 3441 N. Ashland Avenue, Chicago, Illinois 60657.

Copyright © 2005 Loyola Press.
All rights reserved. No part of this book may be reproduced, stored in a retrieval system, or transmitted in any form or by any means, electronic, mechanical, photocopying, recording, or otherwise, without the prior permission of the publisher.

Imprimatur	*Nihil Obstat*
Most Reverend Edwin M. Conway, D.D.	Reverend John G. Lodge, S.S.L., S.T.D.
Vicar General	Censor Deputatus
Archdiocese of Chicago	July 22, 2004
July 23, 2004	

The *Nihil Obstat* and *Imprimatur* are official declarations that a book is free of doctrinal and moral error. No implication is contained therein that those who have granted the *Nihil Obstat* and *Imprimatur* agree with the content, opinions, or statements expressed.

Scripture excerpts are from the New Revised Standard Version Bible, © 1989, Division of Christian Education of the National Council of the Churches of Christ in the United States of America. Used by permission. All rights reserved. Subheadings in Scripture quotations have been added by Kevin Perrotta.

Excerpts from the Vatican conciliar, postconciliar, and papal documents are from the official translations, Libreria Editrice Vaticana, 00120 Citta del Vaticano.

20–21 The Latin text of *Veni, Sancte Spiritus* can be found in Matthew Britt, ed., *The Hymns of the Breviary and Missal* (New York: Benziger Brothers, 1924). Translation by Kevin Perrotta.

32–33 Catherine de Hueck Doherty's quotation is from her book *Fragments of My Life* (Notre Dame, IN: Ave Maria Press, 1979).

44–45 A Latin rendering of St. Ephrem's commentary on Acts can be found in Frederick C. Conybeare, "The Commentary of Ephrem on Acts" in F.J. Foakes Jackson and Kirsopp Lake, eds., *The Beginnings of Christianity*, pt. 1, *The Acts of the Apostles*, vol. 3, *The Text of Acts* (London: Macmillan and Co., 1925). Translation by Kevin Perrotta.

55 Cardinal Léon Joseph Suenens's prayer is translated by Louise M. Perrotta. A French version is available in Karl-Heinz Fleckenstein, *Pour l'Eglise de demain: conversation avec le cardinal Suenens* (Paris: Nouvelle Cité, 1979).

68–69 A Latin version of St. John Chrysostom's homilies on Acts can be found in J.P. Migne, ed., *Patrologia Graeca*, vol. 60 (Paris, 1862). Translation by Kevin Perrotta.

Cover and Interior Design: Th!nk Design Group

ISBN 0-8294-2085-1

Printed in the United States of America

07 08 Bang 5 4 3

Contents

How to Use This Guide

Vou might compare this volume to a short visit to a national park. The park is so large that you could spend months, even years, getting to know it. But a brief visit, if carefully planned, can be worthwhile. In a few hours you can drive through the park and pull over at a handful of sites. At each stop you can get out of the car, take a short trail through the woods, listen to the wind blowing in the trees, get a feel for the place.

In this volume we'll travel through the Acts of the Apostles, making half a dozen stops along the way. At those points we'll proceed on foot, taking a leisurely walk through the selected passages. The readings have been chosen to take us to the heart of the book's message. After each discussion, we'll get back in the car and take the highway to the next stop. "Between Discussions" pages summarize the portions of Acts that we will pass along the way.

This guide provides everything you need to explore Acts of the Apostles in six discussions—or to do a six-part exploration on your own. The introduction on page 6 will prepare you to get the most out of your reading. The weekly sections feature key passages from Acts, with explanations that highlight what these words mean for us today. Equally important, each section supplies questions that will launch you into fruitful discussion, helping you both to explore Acts for yourself and to learn from one another. If you're using the guide by yourself, the questions will spur your personal reflection.

Each discussion is meant to be a *guided discovery*.

Guided ~ None of us is equipped to read the Bible without help. We read the Bible *for* ourselves but not *by* ourselves. Scripture was written to be understood and applied in and with the Church. So each week "A Guide to the Reading" supplies background and explanations. The guide will help you grasp the book's message. Think of it as a friendly park ranger who points out noteworthy details and explains what you're looking at so you can appreciate things for yourself.

Discovery ~ The purpose is for *you* to interact with Acts. "Questions for a Closer Look" is a tool to help you dig into the book and examine it carefully. "Questions for Application" will help you consider what Acts means for your life here and now. Each week concludes with an "Approach to Prayer" section that helps you respond to God's Word. Supplementary "Living Tradition" and "Saints in the Making" sections offer the thoughts and experiences of Christians past and present in order to show you what Acts has meant to others—so that you can consider what it might mean for you.

If you are using this guide for individual study, pay special attention to the questions provided for each week (Warm-Up Questions, Questions for a Closer Look, Questions for Application). One advantage of individual study is that you can take all the time you need to consider all the questions. You may also want to read Acts in its entirety. You will find that the "Between Discussions" pages will help you understand the portions of Acts that are not covered in this guide. Take your time making your way through Acts and this accompanying volume: let your reading be an opportunity for Acts to become God's words to you.

A History in Which We Can Share

Introducing the Acts of the Apostles

The philosopher George Santayana wrote that "those who cannot remember the past are condemned to repeat it." According to this view, the reason for studying history is to learn about the errors people made in the past in order to avoid committing those errors again. This kind of study happened after the atrocities of the Holocaust in Nazi Germany. Scholars and historians studied the Holocaust to figure out how something like that could have happened.

Saint Luke, who wrote the history of the early Church called Acts of the Apostles, saw another purpose for remembering the past. If asked for his view, he would probably have said that those who are ignorant of the past cannot play their part in the present. Luke wrote his history to help his friend Theophilus better understand the origins of the Church and of the Gospel that Luke had received (1:1; unless otherwise noted, all Scripture references in this volume are to Acts). Theophilus would then be prepared to take part in the Church's life and mission.

World leaders have been urged to remember the Holocaust so that such genocide will never occur again. Luke, on the other hand, wanted Theophilus to learn the lessons of the Church in Jerusalem, Joppa, Antioch, and Philippi so as to *continue* living the same life that the first Christians began to live when the Holy Spirit came to them.

Luke probably wrote around the year A.D. 80, and 19 centuries later his history can serve the same purpose for us. Acts of the Apostles puts us in touch with the foundational events of the Church to which we belong. By understanding our history, we can enter more deeply into it. The first Christians' situation was quite different from our situation today, but we can share their experience. God calls us to open ourselves to the same Spirit, to practice the same mutual love and to carry out the same mission that we read about in Luke's history. Luke wants us to know that those who remember the past are enabled to repeat it.

The book that Luke wrote ~ If Luke could examine one of our Bibles today, he might be surprised to find that the two parts of his work are not placed together in the New Testament. Part one, Luke's Gospel, is grouped with the Gospels of Matthew, Mark, and John. Part two, Acts of the Apostles, is placed after the Gospels. In this arrangement, the two sections of Luke's work are separated by the Gospel of John.

There are good reasons for this arrangement: putting all four Gospels together at the beginning of the New Testament indicates the central importance of Jesus himself. But when reading Acts we should keep in mind that the two parts of Luke's work go together. Luke wrote a two-volume history because he was describing a two-stage action of God. When we view the two volumes of the story together, we get a better understanding of how the two stages of God's action are related to each other.

Luke tells the following story in his two-stage work. God had given the people of Israel a special relationship with himself and had promised that he would rescue them from oppression. He fulfilled this promise through Jesus of Nazareth, his Son. God made himself powerfully present to people through Jesus' teaching, miracles, reconciliation of sinners, and inclusion of outcasts. When Jesus accepted a painful death in obedience to God's plans, God raised him from death and placed him in authority over all things. That was stage one, the Gospel of Luke. In stage two, Acts of the Apostles, God sent the Holy Spirit to Jesus' followers. The Spirit enabled them to continue in the way of forgiveness, humility, and care for the needy that Jesus had begun. The Spirit gave them the strength to invite people everywhere to join in this graced life by believing in Jesus.

There are similarities between the two stages. Just as God sent his Son Jesus to make his kingdom present in the world, God has now sent his Spirit to Jesus' followers, who are to extend the presence of his kingdom. Just as God confirmed Jesus' announcement of the kingdom with powerful signs, he now gives signs that confirm the Church's message about Jesus. Jesus had to suffer to accomplish God's purposes; the members of the Church will also have to suffer as they carry out their mission.

It is clear from this summary of Luke's two-part narrative that the principal actor in the whole drama is God. God exercises the initiative. God unfolds a grand plan, first through Jesus, then through the Church. This in turn, highlights the importance of the Church. By his Spirit, God continues through the Church the work that he began through Jesus. The Church is not an afterthought, not a mere human attempt to remember Jesus. The Church is God's instrument in the world.

Acts is a history, but we need to be clear about the type of history it is. In Luke's culture, history writers would often reshape their material in order to bring out the meaning of events for their readers. Scholars who have examined Luke's work closely have found many indications of the historical nature of his reports. Yet in many ways Luke told his story in such a way as to convey his theology of the Spirit and of the Church. We can be confident, then, that in Acts we are getting a fundamentally reliable picture of the early Church. We must be aware, however, that Luke has not tried to present the kind of objectively factual account that would be found in a history textbook.

Acts is full of drama and conflict. ~ In order to appreciate the drama, we need to see the situation of the first Christians from their point of view. Let us imagine that we could travel back to Jerusalem around the year A.D. 30. We arrive in a world that has no international Church. In fact, there are no church buildings or external signs of Christianity at all. No one keeps Sunday as a religious day; no one celebrates Christmas; no one follows a calendar counting years from the birth of Christ.

Let us suppose that we arrive in Jerusalem just after Jesus has finished appearing to his disciples following his Resurrection. He has told them to remain in Jerusalem to wait for the Holy Spirit to come to them. They are now gathered in a spacious home, praying and waiting. There are only about 120 of them, men and women.

All the disciples are Jews, so it makes sense that they have a thoroughly Jewish outlook. If you asked them who Jesus is, they would tell you that he is the Messiah appointed by God to bring liberation and holiness to the people of Israel—and that he now reigns with God. If you asked them what God is doing for Israel through Messiah Jesus, they would say that he is inaugurating the final period of history, the end times, in which he will give saving help to his people. If you looked around the room at the disciples and asked them who they are, they would identify themselves as the renewed community of Israel—the portion of Israel gathered around the Messiah.

Why is it, you might ask them, that Messiah Jesus does not seem to have a program for bringing Jews back to the land of Israel from the foreign lands where most of them live? Why does he not seem to have a program for purifying the Temple so that it might be a place where God's presence is powerfully manifested? Why does he not seem to have a program for freeing the Jews from the oppression of the pagan Romans? In other words, why isn't Jesus doing the things that most Jews are expecting God to accomplish for Israel? The disciples might reply that they themselves have been deeply puzzled by this, but that, while they still have questions, they have begun to grasp that Jesus is fulfilling God's plans for Israel in a different but better way.

The disciples might admit that they don't know what the coming of the Messiah will mean for non-Jews. Jewish expectations on this question varied, and Jesus did not fully clarify the matter for them. If you asked whether non-Jews could join the renewed community of Israel founded by Jesus without being circumcised, the disciples might stare at you in astonishment and stop the interview, thinking that you are no longer interested in asking serious questions.

There is drama and conflict in Acts because God's actions went beyond traditional Jewish understandings of God and Israel. God leads the disciples to bring the message of the expected-but-surprising Messiah Jesus to their fellow Jews. Some Jews accept the message and experience dramatic changes in their lives. Others reject it, and begin to argue with and persecute the disciples. Conflict occurs among the disciples as well, as God leads them to a new understanding of his purposes for Gentiles. (The word *Gentile* refers to any person who is not of the Jewish faith.)

Our reading in Week 1 is all drama. Peter, with the rest of the 12 apostles, appeals to his fellow Jews to change the way they think about Jesus and to recognize him as the promised Messiah. In a remarkable change of heart, thousands of Peter's listeners come to believe in Jesus and join Jesus' community of the renewed Israel. Jesus' salvation gives the new disciples not a nationalistic restoration but a life in the Spirit. A community of believers develops in which men and women experience forgiveness and joy through the Spirit as they worship God together, share a community life, and care for each other's material needs.

Before long, conflict sets in. In Week 2 the apostles' proclamation of Jesus brings them into confrontation with fellow Jews, especially the religious leaders, who do not accept Jesus because he does not fit their expectations for how God will come to save Israel.

Among the Jews of the day was an influential party called the Pharisees, who were known for being strict observers of the Mosaic law. There was much common ground between Jesus and the Pharisees, but many of them reacted against Jesus, for he claimed that God's Kingdom was becoming present through himself. This was a claim that displaced the Mosaic law from its central role in Judaism. When Jesus' followers claimed that he was now risen from the dead and ruling as Messiah and Lord over the final phase of God's dealings with Israel, this struck Pharisees as blasphemous. Many Pharisees hoped that their strict observance of the law would hasten the day when God would grant national restoration to Israel. From their perspective, Jewish Christians' devotion to Jesus was a dangerous diversion.

Our reading in Week 3 shows us a Pharisee named Saul (also called Paul), who puts himself in the forefront of efforts to remove the Christian cancer from the body of Judaism. And then—in one of the most dramatic turnarounds in the entire history of the Church—Jesus appears to Saul and convinces him that Jesus truly has both fulfilled and transcended the expectations of Judaism.

In Week 4 the focus switches to the disciples' own efforts to grasp how Jesus and the Spirit are leading them beyond traditional Jewish expectations. An extraordinary series of actions by the Spirit transports Peter across the religious and cultural divide separating Jews from Gentiles.

Despite the dramatic activity of the Spirit, the idea that Messiah Jesus wishes to be personal Lord over Gentiles is not easy for the disciples to accept. Peter's welcoming of Gentiles directly into the community of the renewed Israel without their first becoming Jews clashes so fundamentally with Jewish expectations that it creates conflict within the Christian community. Thus in Week 5 we read about a council of Church leaders that gathers to figure out what God wants them to do.

Once the Spirit has led the disciples to see that the good news about Jesus goes beyond its Jewish roots and reaches out to all people, the way is open for missionary work. In our final selection, Week 6, we observe Paul's missionary labors among Gentiles. At this point, a new source of conflict appears, as Jewish Christians preaching the one God and his Son Jesus encounter people whose culture is based on belief in many gods.

Questions for modern readers ~ Returning to the 21st century, we reflect on what we have learned. Like the early Jewish followers of Jesus, the Spirit leads us also into drama and conflict. God challenges us to change. He challenges us to move beyond a simplistic childhood understanding of him and develop a mature adult faith. He wishes us to serve him in new ways, and summons us to go beyond our limited expectations of how much we might love, how selflessly we might serve, what suffering we might endure. He wishes us to experience his powerful help as we grow up. He wishes to work through us to make Jesus known. He wishes us to have an influence on the people around us. In all these respects, reading Acts leads us to question our lives and open our hearts to a new cooperation with the Spirit of God.

The Spirit Arrives

Warm-Up Questions

1 On your last birthday, what did you do that was special?

2 Describe a memorable dream. Did it have a message?

3 What was the most important decision you ever made on the spur of the moment? How did it turn out?

Opening the Bible

Acts 2:1–47

Zero Hour of the Christian World Mission

²:¹ When the day of Pentecost had come, they were all together in one place. ² And suddenly from heaven there came a sound like the rush of a violent wind, and it filled the entire house where they were sitting. ³ Divided tongues, as of fire, appeared among them, and a tongue rested on each of them. ⁴ All of them were filled with the Holy Spirit and began to speak in other languages, as the Spirit gave them ability.

⁵ Now there were devout Jews from every nation under heaven living in Jerusalem. ⁶ And at this sound the crowd gathered and was bewildered, because each one heard them speaking in the native language of each. ⁷ Amazed and astonished, they asked, "Are not all these who are speaking Galileans? ⁸ And how is it that we hear, each of us, in our own native language? . . . ¹¹ [I]n our own languages we hear them speaking about God's deeds of power." ¹² All were amazed and perplexed, saying to one another, "What does this mean?" ¹³ But others sneered and said, "They are filled with new wine."

¹⁴ But Peter, standing with the eleven, raised his voice and addressed them, "Men of Judea and all who live in Jerusalem, let this be known to you, and listen to what I say. ¹⁵ Indeed, these are not drunk, as you suppose, for it is only nine o'clock in the morning. ¹⁶ No, this is what was spoken through the prophet Joel:
¹⁷ 'In the last days it will be, God declares,
   that I will pour out my Spirit upon all flesh,
      and your sons and your daughters shall prophesy,
   and your young men shall see visions,
      and your old men shall dream dreams.
¹⁸ Even upon my slaves, both men and women,
      in those days I will pour out my Spirit;
         and they shall prophesy.
¹⁹ And I will show portents in the heaven above
      and signs on the earth below,
         blood, and fire, and smoky mist.
²⁰ The sun shall be turned to darkness
      and the moon to blood,

before the coming of the Lord's great and glorious day. [21] Then everyone who calls on the name of the Lord shall be saved.'

[22] "You that are Israelites, listen to what I have to say: Jesus of Nazareth, a man attested to you by God with deeds of power, wonders, and signs that God did through him among you, as you yourselves know—[23] this man, handed over to you according to the definite plan and foreknowledge of God, you crucified and killed by the hands of those outside the law. [24] But God raised him up, having freed him from death, because it was impossible for him to be held in its power. . . .

[32] "This Jesus God raised up, and of that all of us are witnesses. [33] Being therefore exalted at the right hand of God, and having received from the Father the promise of the Holy Spirit, he has poured out this that you both see and hear. . . . [36] Therefore let the entire house of Israel know with certainty that God has made him both Lord and Messiah, this Jesus whom you crucified."

[37] Now when they heard this, they were cut to the heart and said to Peter and to the other apostles, "Brothers, what should we do?" [38] Peter said to them, "Repent, and be baptized every one of you in the name of Jesus Christ so that your sins may be forgiven; and you will receive the gift of the Holy Spirit. [39] For the promise is for you, for your children, and for all who are far away, everyone whom the Lord our God calls to him." [40] And he testified with many other arguments and exhorted them, saying, "Save yourselves from this corrupt generation." [41] So those who welcomed his message were baptized, and that day about three thousand persons were added. [42] They devoted themselves to the apostles' teaching and fellowship, to the breaking of bread and the prayers.

The Christian Community

[43] Awe came upon everyone, because many wonders and signs were being done by the apostles. [44] All who believed were together and had all things in common; [45] they would sell their possessions and goods and distribute the proceeds to all, as any had need. [46] Day by day, as they spent much time together in the temple, they broke bread at home and ate their food with glad and generous hearts, [47] praising God and having the goodwill of all the people. And day by day the Lord added to their number those who were being saved.

Questions for a Closer Look

1 Which of "God's deeds of power" were the disciples probably speaking about in verse 11? Does Peter's preaching help you answer this question?

2 What is repentance? Why does Peter call people to repent?

3 In a single sentence, how would you summarize Peter's message in verses 16–21? in verses 22–36?

4 What other responses might the crowd have made to Peter's declaration in verses 22–36? Why did they respond as they did?

5 What is the "promise" Peter talks about in verse 39?

6 What sorts of things do people do when the Holy Spirit comes to them (see 2:3–4,41–42)?

A Guide to the Reading

2:1–3 ~ In the large house of a prosperous Jerusalem resident, a half mile or so from the place where Jesus died and rose, 120 of his followers are praying together. They are waiting for Jesus to fulfill a promise he made repeatedly after his Resurrection (1:5,8). Suddenly an explosion of mysterious wind and fire fills the house. Jesus' promise, the Holy Spirit, has arrived. Flames settle above the heads of all 120 disciples: every member of the community receives the Spirit.

The manner of the Spirit's coming recalls the moment, centuries earlier, when God made a covenant with Israel at Mount Sinai. The sound of the wind from heaven that fills the house echoes the frightening noise that announced God's presence at Sinai; the flames reflect God's descent to the mountain in fire. By breathing life into the community of Jesus' followers, God is renewing his covenant with Israel.

The whole people of Israel must be invited to share in this life, and the Spirit has come to enable the disciples to do this task. The flames take the shape of *tongues* because the Spirit will guide the disciples to *speak*. They receive the Spirit not just for their own benefit, but so they might serve others.

2:4–13 ~ We may suppose that the disciples make their way to the courtyards of the Temple, the only place in Jerusalem that can accommodate a large crowd. Jews from all over the world are present. All are astonished to hear the disciples speaking in the visitors' native languages about God's actions (2:6–11). (This is not the same thing as the speaking in unknown languages that other early Christians experienced as a gift of the Spirit, since that speaking in tongues required interpretation.)

2:14–15 ~ Peter, as leader of the apostles, steps forward to offer an explanation. To the accusation that the disciples are drunk, he offers a laid-back response. "Drunk? Before breakfast? Give me a break!"

2:16–21 ~ In a more serious vein, Peter explains that the ability of the disciples to speak in foreign languages shows that God's Spirit has arrived, marking the beginning of a new era in God's dealings with the human race. Peter calls it "the last days." He does not mean that the world is about to end, but that the final period of history has begun. Peter uses cosmic imagery from the prophet Joel not to predict that the world will soon end but to make his listeners aware of what the gift of the Spirit means.

2:22–36 ~ Peter tells his listeners that they were mistaken about Jesus when they demanded his death seven weeks earlier. He explains that through Jesus the new age of God's dealings with the human race was dawning, as his healings and other miracles indicated. Now God has raised Jesus from death and has made him ruler over all things, in fulfillment of a long-standing divine plan.

2:37–40 ~ The crowd is shaken and asks Peter what they should do. "Repent!" he says. The Greek word means "change your mind." They should, of course, repent in the sense of turning away from sin; but first of all they should change their minds about Jesus and then decide to redirect their lives toward him.

Peter's preaching offers a second chance to those of his listeners who had called for Jesus' death. His warning not to let it slip away—"Save yourself from this corrupt generation"—is not a condemnation of the whole world. In Old Testament terminology, the term "corrupt generation" referred especially to people who saw God's mighty acts but then walked away unaffected.

2:41–47 ~ Thousands of men and women accept Peter's message and are baptized—the greatest miracle of Pentecost! There is plenty of water nearby, kept on hand for use in the temple services and for ritual bathing.

The infant Church has now come into existence. It is filled with God's Spirit and guided by the leadership group that gives it continuity with Jesus. A pattern of teaching and prayer, public testimony and mutual care quickly develops. To experience salvation through Jesus means "being added" to this community (2:47).

Questions for Application

1 Peter calls his listeners to change the way they think about Jesus. What is your picture of Jesus? How do you think your picture of Jesus might change as you get older? What might happen in your life that could change your picture of Jesus?

2 In what ways does God give us a second (or third, or 10th) chance in life? What are some things we can do to take advantage of those opportunities?

3 What does it mean to be filled with the Spirit? Do you know someone who seems filled with the Spirit? How do you experience the presence of the Spirit in your life? How can Christians make themselves open to the Spirit?

4 Where in your life (for example, in your family, school, parish, neighborhood) do you see signs of God's activity? How does God call young people to cooperate with what he is doing?

5 What do you find attractive about the church in Jerusalem after Pentecost? What aspects of it offer a model for the Church today? What is the most challenging point in this reading for the Church today? Why?

Approach to Prayer

Listen as a member of the group reads Acts 2:38–39 aloud:

> Peter said to them, "Repent, and be baptized every one of you in the name of Jesus Christ so that your sins may be forgiven; and you will receive the gift of the Holy Spirit. For the promise is for you, for your children, and for all who are far away, everyone whom the Lord our God calls to him."

Pause for a few moments of silent reflection. Close your time together by praying the Our Father.

A Living Tradition

Come, Holy Spirit!

One of the most beautiful medieval Latin hymns may have been written by Innocent III, a 13th-century pope. It is sung every year during Mass on the feast of Pentecost. The prayer is meaningful for everyone, including today's young Catholics.

Come, Holy Spirit. Shine into waiting hearts and minds your radiance bright. Our young hearts and minds are open and ready to receive the light of the Spirit.

Come, you Father of the poor, come, you giver of all store, come, our souls' light. Many of us are "poor" in different ways: hungry for love, lacking the basic necessities of self-confidence and respect for others, socially outcast and spiritually needy. The Spirit is our Father, the one who gives us what we need and lights up our lives.

You, of comforters the best, you, our hearts' dearest guest, in turmoil, kind relief; you, our respite in distress, in the noontime, cool caress, comfort in our grief. It's tough sometimes, this process of maturing into young adults. There are periods of turmoil and moments of distress, and at these times we welcome the comfort of the Spirit.

O Light making all things new, the depths of all who hope in you with yourself fill. Our young lives are filled with new experiences. The Spirit fills us with hope, confidence that God and God's people are leading us in the right direction.

If you should take your grace away, nothing good in us can stay, all turns to ill. We know that we can always rely on the help of the Spirit. Friends and relatives might disappoint us at times, but the Spirit will never let us down.

Wash the grime of sin away, irrigate our barren clay, our illnesses heal; soften every hardened will, thaw the frozen, warm the chill, your ways reveal. We make mistakes, but then we know that the Spirit is there to help us walk away from those mistakes better children of God. With the help of the Spirit, those mistakes will help us grow in our understanding of God's ways.

Give to all your faithful, Lord, to those who trust in your reward, all gifts of grace. Give us all the help we need to be loving and respectful children, hard-working students, faithful friends, and dedicated Catholics.

Give us virtue's blessed goal, give a death that brings us whole before your face. Help us to stay on the road that leads to a holy death. *Amen. Alleluia.*

Between Discussions

I f you are like the rest of us, you look forward to celebrating your birthday every year. You might have cake and ice cream with relatives and friends, and your parents might give you a nice present. Your celebration is forward-looking, focused on your maturing into an adult, but it is also backward-looking, recalling that first moment in your life when you were finally functioning on your own.

The second chapter of Acts is very much like a birth. Pentecost has been called the birthday of the Church, and Luke's account portrays the Church as a kind of newborn infant. We can look at the newborn Church described in the second chapter of Acts and recognize the basic elements that will grow and mature in the centuries to follow. For instance, Luke shows us that the Church is

1. People empowered by the Spirit ~ The Spirit comes to breathe life into Jesus' followers, and there is a burst of activity—marvelous signs of God's presence, inspired preaching, people turning to the Lord, strangers loving one another. We might say that the Church is the group of people among whom the Holy Spirit makes things happen.

2. A community ~ Each person receives the Spirit, but not as isolated individuals; the Spirit comes to a community of people joined in prayer and hope. The Spirit makes the group larger by bringing in many new members and deepens their relationship with each other. Because the members share together in the life of God, they throw their lives open to one another and use their resources to take care of each other.

3. A hierarchical community ~ Before the Spirit comes, Jesus appoints a group of 12 men as leaders. The leader of the leaders, Peter, makes the first public announcement of Jesus' Resurrection. This leadership structure is essential for the community of those who follow Jesus. Jesus entrusted his teaching to these leaders, and they will base the formation of an authentic, Christian community on that teaching.

4. A community on a mission ~ The coming of the Spirit marks the start of Pentecost. This makes possible Peter's preaching about Jesus as Messiah and Lord. As a result of Peter's preaching, thousands of people come to believe in Jesus, are baptized, and join the Church. The miracle of the disciples' speaking in the native languages of the people in the crowd suggests that people of every language and culture will receive the Christian message.

5. A community where everyone plays a part ~ Peter emphasizes that the Spirit is for male and female, young and old, rich and poor. The Church is for everyone, from prominent male apostles to poor widows. Every member contributes to the proclamation of Jesus by helping make it a community of mutual love. The very existence of a community of love that bridges class and social divisions is proof of a divine source of power.

6. A community that worships together ~ The first Christians came together for morning and evening prayers in the Temple and worship in their homes (including the Lord's Supper). This pattern of celebration enabled the mystery of Jesus' life, death, and resurrection to continue to be present among them.

7. A community where Jesus' mother is present ~ Mary is among the disciples at Pentecost. She was already completely open to the action of God's Spirit and was the first to believe in her son. Now she is a sign of faith and hope to the disciples. In the heart of the Church, as fellow disciple and beloved mother of the Lord, she will continue to pray and bear witness to her son in every age.

Healing and Boldness

Warm-Up Questions

1 Describe how a friend helped you when you were in need or in danger. Did you have an opportunity to express your appreciation?

2 Have you ever known someone who experienced a remarkable recovery from illness or injury after prayer, after receiving the Sacrament of the Anointing of the Sick, or after visiting a pilgrimage site such as Lourdes? If so, how did the experience affect the person who was healed? How did it affect you?

THE READING

Acts 3:1–10; 4:5–35

A Crippled Beggar Receives More Than He Asked For

³:¹ One day Peter and John were going up to the temple at the hour of prayer, at three o'clock in the afternoon. ² And a man lame from birth was being carried in. People would lay him daily at the gate of the temple called the Beautiful Gate so that he could ask for alms from those entering the temple. ³ When he saw Peter and John about to go into the temple, he asked them for alms. ⁴ Peter looked intently at him, as did John, and said, "Look at us." ⁵ And he fixed his attention on them, expecting to receive something from them. ⁶ But Peter said, "I have no silver or gold, but what I have I give you; in the name of Jesus Christ of Nazareth, stand up and walk." ⁷ And he took him by the right hand and raised him up; and immediately his feet and ankles were made strong. ⁸ Jumping up, he stood and began to walk, and he entered the temple with them, walking and leaping and praising God. ⁹ All the people saw him walking and praising God, ¹⁰ and they recognized him as the one who used to sit and ask for alms at the Beautiful Gate of the temple; and they were filled with wonder and amazement at what had happened to him. . . .

Interrogation and Threats

⁴:⁵ The next day their rulers, elders, and scribes assembled in Jerusalem, ⁶ with Annas the high priest, Caiaphas, John, and Alexander, and all who were of the high-priestly family. ⁷ When they had made [them] stand in their midst, they inquired, "By what power or by what name did you do this?" ⁸ Then Peter, filled with the Holy Spirit, said to them, "Rulers of the people and elders, ⁹ if we are questioned today because of a good deed done to someone who was sick and are asked how this man has been healed, ¹⁰ let it be known to all of you, and to all the people of Israel, that this man is standing before you in good health by the name of Jesus Christ of Nazareth, whom you crucified, whom God raised from the dead. . . . ¹² There is salvation in no one else,

for there is no other name under heaven given among mortals by which we must be saved."

[13] Now when they saw the boldness of Peter and John and realized that they were uneducated and ordinary men, they were amazed and recognized them as companions of Jesus. [14] When they saw the man who had been cured standing beside them, they had nothing to say in opposition. [15] So they ordered them to leave the council while they discussed the matter with one another. [16] They said, "What will we do with them? For it is obvious to all who live in Jerusalem that a notable sign has been done through them; we cannot deny it. [17] But to keep it from spreading further among the people, let us warn them to speak no more to anyone in this name." [18] So they called them and ordered them not to speak or teach at all in the name of Jesus. [19] But Peter and John answered them, "Whether it is right in God's sight to listen to you rather than to God, you must judge; [20] for we cannot keep from speaking about what we have seen and heard." [21] After threatening them again, they let them go, finding no way to punish them because of the people, for all of them praised God for what had happened. . . .

[23] After they were released, they went to their friends and reported what the chief priests and the elders had said to them. [24] When they heard it, they raised their voices together to God and said, "Sovereign Lord, who made the heaven and the earth, the sea, and everything in them, . . . [29] look at their threats, and grant to your servants to speak your word with all boldness, [30] while you stretch out your hand to heal, and signs and wonders are performed through the name of your holy servant Jesus." [31] When they had prayed, the place in which they were gathered together was shaken; and they were all filled with the Holy Spirit and spoke the word of God with boldness.

Caring for Needy Brothers and Sisters

[32] Now the whole group of those who believed were of one heart and soul, and no one claimed private ownership of any possessions, but everything they owned was held in common. [33] With great power the apostles gave their testimony to the resurrection of the Lord Jesus, and great grace was upon them all. [34] There was not a needy person among them, for as many as owned lands or houses sold them and brought the proceeds of what was sold. [35] They laid it at the apostles' feet, and it was distributed to each as any had need.

Questions for a Closer Look

1 The word *name* is used frequently in this reading. Find the
verses where it occurs. What does the word seem to mean
in these verses? What other word might be substituted for it?

2 Peter speaks of being "saved." Based solely on this week's
and last week's readings, what happened to the first
Christians in Jerusalem when they began to believe in
Jesus? From what were they saved?

3 How is the response to Peter's preaching about Jesus in
chapter 4 (4:13–18,21) different from the response in
chapter 2 (2:37)? What do you think caused the difference?

4 What does Peter's statement in 3:6 tell us about the
leaders of the Christian community in Jerusalem?

5 What do this week's and last week's readings indicate about
Peter's role in the church in Jerusalem?

A Guide to the Reading

3:1 ~ Every morning and midafternoon, laypeople would join the Jewish priests in prayer in the temple courtyard. This is why Peter and John were climbing the steps to the temple mount.

We might think it odd for the Christian leaders to continue participating in Jewish worship. But the first Christians saw what God was doing among them simply as the fulfillment of what he had in mind for Israel. To an outside observer, Jesus' followers would have looked like a renewal movement within Judaism. So Peter and John feel perfectly natural about praying with their fellow Jews in the Temple.

3:2–6 ~ Saint John Chrysostom observed that the unplanned nature of the healing of the paralyzed man suggests that Peter had no ambition to make a name for himself as a healer. Saint Bede pointed out that the fact that the apostles were not carrying any money with them showed they were not dipping into the contributions for the poor that passed through their hands.

3:7–8 ~ Peter grasps the hand that the man continues to hold out for a coin and gives him something better. Saint Ephrem suggested that the man leaped around awkwardly because he had not yet gotten the hang of walking.

3:9—4:4 ~ The sight of the man bounding through the temple courtyard draws a large crowd. Peter makes it clear to them that *he* has not healed the man; Jesus has done it. Peter proclaims that Jesus is the Messiah and appeals to his fellow Jews to turn to Jesus. Temple officials soon show up, annoyed that Peter is preaching about Jesus' Resurrection, and lock up the two apostles for the night.

4:8–12 ~ The next morning, brought before the Temple's governing council, Peter is "filled with the Holy Spirit." This does not refer to a sudden burst of holiness or a spiritual experience but to the help that God is giving him to give testimony to Jesus. In the Catholic tradition this sort of divine assistance is called "actual grace," the grace to take on the action or task at hand.

Peter begins his address respectfully: "Rulers of the people and elders." But then he boldly declares not only that the risen Jesus has healed the man; he goes on to point out the difference between the religious leaders' view of Jesus and God's view of Jesus. Peter wants to make it absolutely clear that Jesus is God's only agent for dealing with the human race.

4:13 ~ The council is astonished by Peter's boldness. We might also be amazed, since we know about Peter's earlier cowardice, when he had intended to follow Jesus courageously but discovered his own weakness (Luke 22:31–34,54–62). Now the Holy Spirit is enabling Peter to be the brave man he wanted to be then.

4:14–18 ~ The council members are unwilling to change their opinion of Jesus, but they cannot deny the healing, so they resort to a form of damage control. The fact that they do not want even to speak his name shows their hostility to Jesus.

4:19–30 ~ Given the temple council's threats, the Christians might easily have decided to lay low or leave town. But instead of running away, the Christians ask God to "grant to your servants to speak your word with all boldness"; in other words, they want to continue doing what they were warned not to do. Their prayer for boldness does not necessarily mean that they *feel* brave, but it does indicate a desire to *be* brave and an awareness that they need God's help.

4:32–35 ~ Another description of the Christian community follows a story about apostolic preaching. The Holy Spirit is working among the first Christians to help them grow stronger and increase in numbers. Notice how the statements about the apostles' public testimonies to Jesus are included in the descriptions of the Christians' care for needy members (4:33). Community life and public testimony are closely related: the proclamation of Jesus is believable because outsiders can see how his followers care for one another. Some members bear witness to Jesus through speech, others through loving service; together they give clear and convincing witness to Jesus.

Questions for Application

1 What are your special gifts? Where are you tempted to use them for yourself rather than for other people? What is something you can do that will encourage you to use your gifts for others?

2 When does being a Christian get in the way of being popular at school or among other young people? What is your experience of this?

3 Peter and John declared that "we cannot keep from speaking about what we have seen and heard" about Jesus. In what ways are you like Peter and John, speaking about what you have seen and heard about Jesus?

4 What has been your experience of actual grace helping you to become the person God created you to be? What are some things you can do to cooperate better with the help given you by the Spirit?

5 Put yourself in the place of the Christians who heard Peter and John's report about how they had been punished for speaking about Jesus. What would *you* then ask God for?

Approach to Prayer

Begin by praying the Our Father aloud with the group. Reflect silently for a few moments and ask the Holy Spirit for courage in bearing witness to Christ or in dealing with weakness or difficulty. Then listen as a member of the group reads the following prayer aloud:

Come, Holy Spirit, fill the hearts of your faithful; enkindle in us the fire of your love. Send forth your Spirit, and we shall be created, and you shall renew the face of the earth. O God, who by the light of your Holy Spirit did instruct the hearts of your faithful, grant that by that same Holy Spirit we may be truly wise and ever rejoice in his consolations, through Jesus Christ our Lord. Amen.

Saints in the Making

Wrestling with the Spirit

In the early 1930s, Catherine de Hueck, a young Russian immigrant living in Toronto, Canada, was struggling to discern what God's will was for her life. Catherine had grown up in an affluent family, but throughout her childhood she felt a desire to be poor. When she was in the first grade, a nun in her school told the class the story of Saint Francis of Assisi and how he gave away his wealth to follow Jesus and serve the poor. "Someday I will be just like him," Catherine said to herself. "I will go and live with the poor."

Catherine and her family fled Communist Russia and came to live in Canada and the United States. She was almost penniless when she arrived, having lost everything in the Communist Revolution, but with intelligence and hard work, she eventually achieved a comfortable life again. But then the desire to be like Francis returned, and she came up with a plan to live and work among Toronto's poorest residents.

Catherine consulted some priests, but they thought that her idea was impractical. The archbishop, Neil McNeil, however, thought there was something to it. He advised Catherine to take a year to pray and consider it.

Looking back four decades later, she wrote that the specific details of that year of discernment were vague in her memory. "I was wrestling with the Spirit—you might almost call me an 'early Pentecostal'! They are wrestlers with the Spirit too. . . . The Archbishop had approved my vocation, generally speaking. . . . What was not so clear was, Should I do it? Should I leave everything behind? Should I sell all I possessed? Should I, or shouldn't I? . . . When you are wrestling with the Spirit like this, the things of the world become slightly remote."

At the end of the year, Catherine was clear enough about God's purposes to take the next step. She quit her high-paying job, gave away her possessions, and went to live in the poorest section of Toronto. Other men and women came to join her, and their community came to be called Friendship House.

The Friendship House in Toronto closed, but some years later, Catherine (who came to be known by her later married name, Catherine Doherty) founded a community in Combermere, Ontario called Madonna House. Catherine died in 1985, but Madonna House continues, in Canada, the United States, and other countries, as a group of laypeople and priests committed to prayer, poverty, and service to the poor.

Between Discussions

Were the early Christians really as charitable toward each other as Luke recounts? As Luke himself shows, the answer is yes and no. On the positive side, Luke cites the example of a man named Joseph Barnabas, who sold his rural property and gave the proceeds to the apostles to give to the poor (4:36–37). On the other hand, a couple named Ananias and Sapphira, who also sold some property, tucked away a portion of the proceeds for themselves while pretending to present all of it to the apostles (5:1–2).

No community rule required members to hand over all their money (5:4); Ananias and Sapphira were wrong not in keeping their money but in lying about it. Their lie seemed to deny that God was present in any special way within the Christian community. What followed, however, revealed the powerful presence of the Spirit. Informed by the Spirit, Peter confronted the couple with their deception and, perhaps from shock and shame, they collapsed and died (5:3–11). The story records a highly unusual instance of God's judgment and does not set a pattern for God's dealings with us. But it reminds us that God is not distant from the Church or ill-informed about what its members are doing.

After some healings, which testify further to the Spirit's presence in the Church (5:12–16), the apostles are again forced to appear before the temple council (5:17–42). The apostles boldly declare their commitment to speak the truth about Jesus. The council gives them a second warning, this time accompanied by a beating.

Back home with their Christian brothers and sisters, the apostles find themselves dealing with a dispute about care for the widows in the community. The Greek-speaking Jewish Christians complain that their widows are receiving less than the widows of the Aramaic-speaking Jewish Christians. The Twelve propose that the members of the community select men from among the Greek-speaking wing of the community to help remedy the problem, and seven are chosen (6:1–6).

The most common opinion is that these men were, in effect, deacons, whose commission was to administer care for the poor. Luke, however, does not portray them as functioning this way. In fact, the Seven act like the apostles, preaching and working miracles (chapters 7 and 8). Another possible view is that the Seven were chosen to extend the leadership of the Twelve: the Seven are to lead the Jewish Christians who are culturally Greek, while the Twelve lead those who are culturally Semitic. If this is the case, the ordination of the Seven gives us insight into how the Twelve passed on their authority in an orderly way to the next generation of Christian leaders.

The ordination of leaders for the Greek-speaking Jewish Christians is an example of how the Church strives to function in different cultures while maintaining unity in the faith. The Church has always included people who come from different cultures and social classes and who speak different languages. This means that the Church has always experienced the tensions that arise from people having different perspectives and viewpoints.

The apostles have been given two warnings to stop preaching about Jesus. In Jewish practice, after two warnings comes punishment. As it turns out, it is one of the Seven, Stephen, who suffers the penalty for speaking about Jesus. In a lengthy speech to the temple council, Stephen reminds his listeners of God's dealings with upright men in the past—Abraham, Joseph, and Moses—and points to Jesus as *the* Upright One whom God has sent in their own day to complete God's plans for Israel. Stephen criticizes the religious leaders for presuming that they have God boxed up in the Temple and thus missing his supreme representative, Jesus.

Stephen's accusation provokes a riot. He is dragged out of the city and stoned to death. His dying words are a prayer for God to forgive his attackers. Just as Jesus forgave his executioners from the cross, Stephen calls down God's mercy on those who are stoning him.

Who Are You, Lord?

Warm-Up Questions

1 Going back and forth to school is pretty routine business. Have you ever had any surprises along the way?

2 How do you feel about being criticized or made fun of by someone (parent, teacher, friend)? What is the best way to handle criticism? Has people's criticism of you helped you to grow?

3 When you meet someone for the first time, does that person's race, looks, clothes, or manner of speech sometimes get in the way of your warming up to them?

Opening the Bible

What's Happened

Stephen, a leader among the Christians in Jerusalem, dies as the first Christian martyr—the first follower of Jesus to lose his life through "bearing witness" to his Lord. Among those who join in the lynching: a man named Saul.

THE READING

Acts 8:1,3; 9:1–30

Jesus Reveals Himself to a Persecutor

[8:1] That day a severe persecution began against the church in Jerusalem, and all except the apostles were scattered throughout the countryside of Judea and Samaria. . . . [3] Saul was ravaging the church by entering house after house; dragging off both men and women, he committed them to prison. . . .

[9:1] Saul, still breathing threats and murder against the disciples of the Lord, went to the high priest [2] and asked him for letters to the synagogues at Damascus, so that if he found any who belonged to the Way, men or women, he might bring them bound to Jerusalem. [3] Now as he was going along and approaching Damascus, suddenly a light from heaven flashed around him. [4] He fell to the ground and heard a voice saying to him, "Saul, Saul, why do you persecute me?" [5] He asked, "Who are you, Lord?" The reply came, "I am Jesus, whom you are persecuting. [6] But get up and enter the city, and you will be told what you are to do." [7] The men who were traveling with him stood speechless because they heard the voice but saw no one. [8] Saul got up from the ground, and though his eyes were open, he could see nothing; so they led him by the hand and brought him into Damascus. [9] For three days he was without sight, and neither ate nor drank.

A Conversion That No One Expected

[10] Now there was a disciple in Damascus named Ananias. The Lord said to him in a vision, "Ananias." He answered, "Here I am,

Lord." [11] The Lord said to him, "Get up and go to the street called Straight, and at the house of Judas look for a man of Tarsus named Saul. At this moment he is praying, [12] and he has seen in a vision a man named Ananias come in and lay his hands on him so that he might regain his sight." [13] But Ananias answered, "Lord, I have heard from many about this man, how much evil he has done to your saints in Jerusalem; [14] and here he has authority from the chief priests to bind all who invoke your name." [15] But the Lord said to him, "Go, for he is an instrument whom I have chosen to bring my name before Gentiles and kings and before the people of Israel; [16] I myself will show him how much he must suffer for the sake of my name." [17] So Ananias went and entered the house. He laid his hands on Saul and said, "Brother Saul, the Lord Jesus, who appeared to you on your way here, has sent me so that you may regain your sight and be filled with the Holy Spirit." [18] And immediately something like scales fell from his eyes, and his sight was restored. Then he got up and was baptized, [19] and after taking some food, he regained his strength.

For several days he was with the disciples in Damascus, [20] and immediately he began to proclaim Jesus in the synagogues, saying, "He is the Son of God." [21] All who heard him were amazed and said, "Is not this the man who made havoc in Jerusalem among those who invoked this name? And has he not come here for the purpose of bringing them bound before the chief priests?" [22] Saul became increasingly more powerful and confounded the Jews who lived in Damascus by proving that Jesus was the Messiah.

[23] After some time had passed, the Jews plotted to kill him, [24] but their plot became known to Saul. They were watching the gates day and night so that they might kill him; [25] but his disciples took him by night and let him down through an opening in the wall, lowering him in a basket.

[26] When he had come to Jerusalem, he attempted to join the disciples; and they were all afraid of him, for they did not believe that he was a disciple. [27] But Barnabas took him, brought him to the apostles, and described for them how on the road he had seen the Lord, who had spoken to him, and how in Damascus he had spoken boldly in the name of Jesus. [28] So he went in and out among them in Jerusalem, speaking boldly in the name of the Lord. [29] He spoke and argued with the Hellenists; but they were attempting to kill him. [30] When the believers learned of it, they brought him down to Caesarea and sent him off to Tarsus.

Questions for a Closer Look

1 Why does Jesus say to Saul, "Why do you persecute me?" rather than "Why do you persecute *my followers*?" [italics added]? What does Jesus' choice of words tell us about his relationship with his followers?

2 What do you suppose Saul did or thought during his days of blindness before Ananias came to him? What purpose might this period have served for Saul?

3 Why didn't God restore Saul's sight directly rather than through Ananias?

4 Judging just from this reading, in what ways did Saul's conversion change him? In what ways did he remain the same person?

5 In portrayals of Saul's conversion, artists usually depict him being knocked off his horse when Jesus appears to him. What's wrong with this picture?

A Guide to the Reading

8:1–3 ~ If Luke had recorded the stoning of Stephen with a camcorder instead of a pen, he would probably have panned through the crowd until his camera came to rest on a face filled with anger—the face of Saul of Tarsus. Saul is the first known organizer of an anti-Christian persecution. After Stephen's death, Saul, driven by what seem to have been strong feelings of violent anger, leads a concerted effort to destroy the Christian community.

Like many other Pharisees, Saul probably reacted with hostility to Jesus because Jesus rejected the Pharisees' concept of Israel as a community that would strictly observe their interpretations of the Mosaic law in the hope that God would bring national vindication. Saul was his Semitic name. He is better known by his Greco-Roman name, Paul (which is what we shall call him from now on).

9:1–7 ~ Paul tries to spread the persecution to Damascus, a Syrian city 135 miles north of Jerusalem. As he nears Damascus, a light flashes around him and a voice cries out his name. When Paul asks who the person is, the speaker gives a terrifying answer: "I am Jesus." The man whom Paul thought was dead is alive! And he is well aware of Paul's hostility to him: "Why do you persecute me?" Yet Jesus has not revealed himself in order to crush Paul but to get him to change his mind. Jesus has work in mind for this persecutor of his followers.

9:8–9 ~ Paul gets up from the ground unable to see. His blindness is not a punishment but a sign of his helplessness before the power of the one he had been opposing. He does not eat or drink, perhaps because he is seeking God, or perhaps because he has been completely overwhelmed by his encounter with Jesus.

9:10–16 ~ Ananias offers God some information about Paul (hasn't God heard why Paul was coming to Damascus?) God does not seem annoyed by Ananias's objection, but enters into a real conversation with his servant. In the end though, God does insist on being obeyed.

9:17–19 ~ Ananias would have been among those whom Paul had planned to cart off to prison in Jerusalem. It must have been humbling for Paul to realize that the Lord was using one of Paul's intended victims to receive him into the Christian community.

A special revelation brought Paul to recognize Jesus and end his persecution of Jesus' followers. But now Paul receives the Spirit and becomes a member of the Church through Baptism. No matter how directly God may reveal himself to a person, conversion to Jesus is completed only by becoming a member of his body.

Paul's conversion is unusually dramatic, yet it involves aspects of God's dealings that many other people have experienced. Paul did not seek Jesus; Jesus sought Paul. Paul learned that Jesus had been present with him even when Paul did not yet know him, even when Paul rejected him. God dealt with Paul in a way that fit in with Paul's particular needs and personality: Paul was a violent persecutor, so he was given a violent confrontation with the truth. God showed Paul that he had a plan for Paul's life, a plan that Paul could discover only by recognizing his own blindness, by coming to grips with who Jesus is, and by deciding to follow him.

9:20–25 ~ This was the first time in biblical history that God called into his service someone who had persecuted his people. Thus God's calling and commissioning of Paul is a striking display of divine mercy. We see reflected in Paul's life a God who calls sinners great and small. God calls them not only to forgiveness and reconciliation with himself but also to play a role in advancing his kingdom of forgiveness and reconciliation.

9:26–30 ~ Jerusalem is the center of opposition to the Christian movement. So Paul's visit to Jerusalem illustrates his continuing boldness. And, since the apostles are in Jerusalem, Paul's interest in visiting the city also shows that he wants to keep in touch with the "mother church." The unity that the Spirit began to give the Church on Pentecost continues to be embodied in new ways as the Christian movement spreads out and grows in numbers.

Questions for Application

1 Paul experienced a period of blindness before his Baptism. Have there been times in your life when you have felt you were blind, feeling negative towards life in general? Why does God sometimes use such periods to help us grow as persons? What is the best way to deal with such experiences?

2 Do you believe that God has specifically chosen you to play some part in his purposes in the world? What are some things you can do to find out what that part is?

3 Drawing on your own experience and that of people you know, as well as on the story of Paul, what does conversion to Christ mean? In what ways can a person who already believes in God experience conversion?

4 What people in your life have played the role of Ananias, welcoming you into the life of the Church and praying for you? What can you learn from these people? How can you imitate them?

5 Paul immediately began to share the knowledge of Jesus he had received. How can you share with others the spiritual and material resources God has given you?

Approach to Prayer

Listen as a member of the group reads aloud 9:1–6. Then pray silently that young men and women like yourselves will hear God's call to conversion, especially those who seem to be in special need of God's grace and help. Reread aloud Acts 9:1–6. Then as a group pray this prayer to Saint Paul.

Saint Paul, once a persecutor of the Church and then an apostle of Christ, God shone his light on you to show you that you were traveling on the wrong road. He treated you mercifully when you were behaving as his enemy. By your preaching, you brought the good news of God's forgiveness and grace to many people. Now by your prayers may God's kindness and truth come to these for whom we pray, for the glory of God. Amen.

A Living Tradition

Humbled by God

The earliest known Christian teacher to write about Acts was Saint Ephrem the Syrian, a deacon who lived in Nisibis, in modern southeast Turkey, in the fourth century. After you have read his thoughts on Paul's dramatic conversion, think about your own dedication to spreading the Good News of the risen Lord.

Saul was more violently opposed to the Church than even the priests were. On his own initiative he went and obtained a decree from them against the Christians and set out to persecute them. But out of consideration for the Church, God made Saul a disciple before he could carry out all the persecution he strove to accomplish.

God blinded Saul with light and terrified him. Saul fell to the ground. Before the voice spoke, he lay there stunned, wondering who had struck him from heaven—not having any idea that it was Jesus, because he did not think Jesus was risen from the dead. When a voice asked him, "Saul, why do you persecute me?" Saul was thrown into confusion. He thought to himself, I am persecuting on behalf of heaven. How can I be persecuting him who dwells in heaven? So Saul said, "Who are you, my Lord, who endure persecution in heaven? I persecute Jesus, who is among the dead, with his disciples." Then the Lord said to him, "I am Jesus, whom you are persecuting!"

Saul was terror-stricken by this. He was very much afraid that he might not ever get up from the earth where he was thrown, that he might never see the light of day again. His teeth were chattering with fear at the thought of punishment too great to bear. So he asked, "Lord, what do you want me to do? For whatever I have done up until now, I did in ignorance. Let me become your preacher, so that I might make amends for my persecution."

Nevertheless, God did not heal him on the spot, but had him come into Damascus blinded, so that all in the city might come and see him, and take warning from the sign that was imposed on him. Taking him by the hands, his companions led him into Damascus, to which he had set out with such great arrogance. The man who had come to the city to bind up and draw out others was himself drawn into the city like one bound up.

Between Discussions

Paul returns home for a short while (9:28–30), but he will soon reemerge to become the great evangelizer of the Gentiles. He will not, however, be the first to penetrate the religious and cultural barrier between Jews and Gentiles. The Christian mission's breakthrough into the non-Jewish world will come through Peter, as we will read next week (chapter 10). All the missionary work that follows, throughout the world and into our own time, will stem from the pioneer witness-bearing of Peter, the leader of the apostles. The Church, growing and spreading, remains in continuity with its beginnings in Jesus' chosen group of apostles, who were witnesses of his life, death, and resurrection.

Here is how the breakthrough happens. Peter leaves Jerusalem to visit the Jewish-Christian communities that may have been founded by Philip, one of the Seven (8:40). In the town of Lydda, Peter heals a man named Aeneas who has been bedridden for eight years. In the nearby town of Joppa, he raises from death a woman named Tabitha, or Dorcas (9:32–43). In both his Gospel and in Acts, Luke often reports miracles in pairs of stories, one dealing with a man, the other with a woman. This pattern seems to be Luke's way of showing that the Good News is for everyone, both men and women.

Peter works a series of wonders and signs (3:1–6; 5:14–16). Further miracles will follow in the ministry of Paul (14:8–10; 20:7–12). Miraculous healings and restorations of life were a big part of the ministry of the first leaders of the Church. Such extraordinary phenomena naturally attracted attention and gave Christians an opening to talk about Jesus. But the miracles were not just attention-getters or expressions of God's love for the few individuals who directly benefited. Jesus worked healings as a sign that God's Kingdom was becoming present in the world through him. The fact that the same miraculous signs would continue through his followers shows that Jesus' death and resurrection has brought us into the final age in God's relationship with men and women.

The early Christians welcomed healings as a way of helping other people recognize God's mercy through Jesus. But they did not expect that these powerful signs of God's presence would make their own lives easy. Healings did not make Peter and Paul wealthy. They helped make Peter and Paul well known, but the healings also involved the two men in dangerous disputes with political and religious authorities (chapters 3–4). Thus the Christians prayed not only for miracles but also for courage to speak boldly and accept their share of suffering.

Readers might take note of both expectations. The early Christians expected that God would display his mercy to people in extraordinary ways. And they expected that they themselves would encounter hardships in the course of making Jesus known. How do their expectations compare with our own? Are we as open as they were to the Spirit's acting in powerful and unpredictable ways? Do we pray for the courage to face difficulties in Christ's service? Most of us would prefer safe routines without suffering. But reading Acts reminds us that God has greater and nobler expectations for our lives.

After the incidents with Aeneas and Tabitha, Peter stays on in the home of a tanner in Joppa, on the Mediterranean coast, in the vicinity of modern Tel Aviv. He has reached the edge of Jewish settlement in Palestine; north of Joppa, the towns along the coast are mostly Gentile. There is a kind of theological geography in Luke's account. Peter has come to a religious and cultural borderland. The gospel has spread up to that border; will it now cross over into the Gentile world?

Peter would have been very reluctant to carry the gospel across the boundary. The Jewish consciousness of having been chosen by God and called to a special way of life erected a barrier between Jews and the rest of the world. Left to himself, Peter probably would have continued to bring the announcement of the Jewish Messiah only to fellow Jews. But Peter was not going to be left to himself.

The Spirit Leads the Way

Warm-Up Questions

1 What is the most surprising thing that has ever happened during a class?

2 How do you react when someone interrupts you while you are speaking?
- ○ I keep right on talking.
- ○ I meekly give way.
- ○ I let the other person speak, but I show my annoyance.
- ○ I feel annoyed, but try not to show it.
- ○ I listen to the other person, but try to complete my thought.

Opening the Bible

Acts 10:1–48

Complementary Visions

[10:1] In Caesarea there was a man named Cornelius, a centurion of the Italian Cohort, as it was called. [2] He was a devout man who feared God with all his household; he gave alms generously to the people and prayed constantly to God. [3] One afternoon at about three o'clock he had a vision in which he clearly saw an angel of God coming in and saying to him, "Cornelius." [4] He stared at him in terror and said, "What is it, Lord?" He answered, "Your prayers and your alms have ascended as a memorial before God. [5] Now send men to Joppa for a certain Simon who is called Peter. . . . " [7] When the angel who spoke to him had left, he called two of his slaves and a devout soldier from the ranks of those who served him, [8] and after telling them everything, he sent them to Joppa.

[9] About noon the next day, as they were on their journey and approaching the city, Peter went up on the roof to pray. [10] He became hungry and wanted something to eat; and while it was being prepared, he fell into a trance. [11] He saw the heaven opened and something like a large sheet coming down, being lowered to the ground by its four corners. [12] In it were all kinds of four-footed creatures and reptiles and birds of the air. [13] Then he heard a voice saying, "Get up, Peter; kill and eat." [14] But Peter said, "By no means, Lord; for I have never eaten anything that is profane or unclean." [15] The voice said to him again, a second time, "What God has made clean, you must not call profane." [16] This happened three times, and the thing was suddenly taken up to heaven.

[17] Now while Peter was greatly puzzled about what to make of the vision that he had seen, suddenly the men sent by Cornelius appeared. They . . . were standing by the gate. . . . [23] So Peter invited them in and gave them lodging.

The next day he got up and went with them, and some of the believers from Joppa accompanied him. [24] The following day they came to Caesarea. Cornelius was expecting them and had called together his relatives and close friends. [25] On Peter's arrival Cornelius met him, . . . [27] [a]nd as he talked with him, he went in and found that many had assembled; [28] and he said to them, "You yourselves know that it is unlawful for a Jew to associate with or to visit a Gentile; but God has shown me that I should not call anyone profane or unclean. [29] So when I was sent for, I came without objection. Now may I ask why you sent for me?"

[30] Cornelius replied, "Four days ago at this very hour, at three o'clock, I was praying in my house when suddenly a man in dazzling clothes stood before me. [31] He said, 'Cornelius, your prayer has been heard and your alms have been remembered before God. [32] Send therefore to Joppa and ask for Simon, who is called Peter. . . .' [33] Therefore I sent for you immediately, and you have been kind enough to come. So now all of us are here in the presence of God to listen to all that the Lord has commanded you to say."

The Gentile Pentecost

[34] Then Peter began to speak to them: "I truly understand that God shows no partiality, [35] but in every nation anyone who fears him and does what is right is acceptable to him. [36] You know the message he sent to the people of Israel, preaching peace by Jesus Christ. . . . [38] how God anointed Jesus of Nazareth with the Holy Spirit and with power; how he went about doing good and healing all who were oppressed by the devil, for God was with him. [39] We are witnesses to all that he did both in Judea and in Jerusalem. They put him to death by hanging him on a tree; [40] but God raised him on the third day and allowed him to appear, [41] not to all the people but to us who were chosen by God as witnesses, and who ate and drank with him after he rose from the dead. [42] He commanded us to preach to the people and to testify that he is the one ordained by God as judge of the living and the dead. [43] All the prophets testify about him that everyone who believes in him receives forgiveness of sins through his name."

[44] While Peter was still speaking, the Holy Spirit fell upon all who heard the word. [45] The circumcised believers who had come with Peter were astounded that the gift of the Holy Spirit had been poured out even on the Gentiles, [46] for they heard them speaking in tongues and extolling God. Then Peter said, [47] "Can anyone withhold the water for baptizing these people who have received the Holy Spirit just as we have?" [48] So he ordered them to be baptized in the name of Jesus Christ. Then they invited him to stay for several days.

Questions for a Closer Look

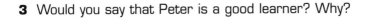

1 Who takes the initiative in this episode?

2 What picture of Cornelius do you get from what he says and does as well as from what is said about him? In what ways is he a model for believers in God?

3 Would you say that Peter is a good learner? Why?

4 If God was going to speak to Cornelius and Peter so directly and clearly, why didn't he let either of them know fully what he intended to do?

5 What is the climax of the episode? What makes this climax so important?

A Guide to the Reading

10:1–8 ~ Cornelius is a noncommissioned officer in the Roman army. His unit, the Italian Cohort, is known to have been an auxiliary contingent of archers. He is described as "a devout man who feared God," which means that he is a Gentile who worships the God of Israel and leads an upright life but has not joined the Jewish people by being circumcised. Since he is not Jewish, he cannot offer sacrifice in the temple. But, an angel lets him know that God finds his prayers and generosity to the poor as pleasing as a Jew's sacrifice.

10:9–17 ~ Peter goes up to pray on the flat roof of the house, which may have been the only escape from a noisy household. He is confronted with a vision of food and what may be the most difficult issue he has ever had to deal with.

The Mosaic food regulations required Jews to be different from other people. This clearly identified Jews as a people in a special relationship with God. Erasing the food laws would make Jews more like Gentiles, something that would be almost impossible for a devout first-century Jew to accept. There are stories in the Old Testament of Jews who died rather than violate the dietary laws. At this point in Acts, the Christians are Jews and assume that God still wants Israel to be different from other peoples. The blessings of Messiah Jesus are for Israel—and for Gentiles only if they attach themselves to Israel. But the voice in the vision announces to Peter that God has stopped making a distinction between clean and unclean animals. How can that be, Peter wonders. He faces the enormous challenge of rethinking the foundations of his religion, and he struggles to understand what his Lord is about.

10:23–33 ~ God has given Cornelius and Peter matching visions. He speaks to the two men separately not to make them independent but precisely in order to bring them together. To each man, God speaks only part of his message. The two men have to put their two pieces of the puzzle together in order to see the whole picture of what God is about.

From Peter's retelling of his vision to Cornelius, we can see that Peter understood its meaning. He knew that he would be able to enter as a guest into Cornelius's house because God no longer meant for him to consider any human being unclean by nature.

Cornelius's explanation brings Peter to the next stage of insight. Peter learns that God finds Cornelius acceptable. Not only has God removed the barrier between Jews and Gentiles, he has prepared the Gentiles for the good news about Jesus. Peter can now offer the gospel to Cornelius as he had been offering it to Jews in Jerusalem.

10:34–43 ~ Peter presents the gospel in outline to Cornelius, his family, friends, and military and business associates. Luke had recorded in his Gospel the angel's message to the unclean shepherds about peace to people of goodwill. Cornelius and company are the men and women of goodwill to whom God's peace is about to come.

10:44–48 ~ Cornelius and his household believe Peter's message about Jesus, and the Spirit comes to them. They are inspired to burst out in praises of God, as the first disciples had done at Pentecost. Since God has accepted these Gentiles as believers in his Son, Peter feels he has no choice but to acknowledge them as brothers and sisters in Christ and receive them into the Church through Baptism. Cornelius and his household are baptized without circumcision—without becoming Jews.

The Gospel has leaped the barrier and is loose in the world.

Questions for Application

1 Which people or events have helped you most in your own process of learning to follow the Lord?

2 Teenagers are often resistant to what they are told by parents, teachers, and other adults. What are the good and bad sides of such resistance when it comes to their relationships with God?

3 What gifts for serving others has God given you? How do you plan on using those gifts? How might you be able to fit your efforts together with those of others in the Church in order to accomplish God's purposes?

4 How can a person strike a balance between holding on to what is good and true and being open to change? As you grow older, how can you remain open to learning about God and responding to him in new ways?

5 How is it helpful for you to discuss your faith with other Christians?

6 There are things groups can do to be more welcoming to a wider variety of people. Is your school doing any of these things? your family? your parish? your youth group? your circle of friends?

Approach to Prayer

Pray along silently as a member of the group reads aloud this prayer of Cardinal Léon Joseph Suenens, a Belgian cardinal who was one of the leading figures at the Second Vatican Council.

Lord, give us the
breath of life
so that we will not
run out of breath
along the way,
so that our lungs
may always be filled
with bracing air
to help us advance
towards tomorrow
without looking back
or counting the cost . . .
Breath to hope anew,
As if life were
beginning this very
morning,
to hope against wind
and tides
because of your
presence and your
promise . . .
Your breath . . .
the Spirit who blows
where he will,
in gusts
or bursts of wind
or with that
light touch
by which you invite
us to follow
your inspirations.
Amen.

Saints in the Making

Moved by the Spirit
By Gerald Darring

My son Andy graduated from Loyola University New Orleans in May 1989. He immediately went into the Jesuit Volunteer Corps, a Catholic lay volunteer organization dedicated to promoting social justice, and ended up spending a year in Bethel, a town in southwestern Alaska. His task was to work with young Yupik Eskimos, who were experiencing culture shock over the clash with modern reality. At the beginning of the 20th century, the Yupik people were living simple lives, no different from the lives they had led for centuries. Now they were being overwhelmed with color TVs and microwaves, and they were having a hard time adjusting. The suicide rate for the Yupik people was the highest of any group in the United States.

Andy would spend a week in a village teaching elementary, middle, and high school students such things as self esteem, personal health, and sexuality. He would return to Bethel for the weekend, and then the next week he was off to another village. It was a heart-wrenching experience as he tried to help the young Yupiks deal with such problems as alcohol, drugs, and various forms of abuse.

As the year was coming to an end, he decided to travel with a Jesuit priest along the Yukon River in a sort of retreat, which would give Andy the chance to reflect on what he had experienced in Alaska. One day, while they were in the town of Pilot Station, a young Yupik, who had just graduated from high school, got drunk, and for whatever reason, climbed to the top of an abandoned windmill. Something happened, and the young man fell to his death. Andy was caught up in the family grieving, and during a break in the funeral events, he went out into the family's back yard and started picking up little pieces of things that had been left behind after the spring thaw. Before he knew it, he was putting the small items together into some kind of shape, and when it was done, Andy was holding a cross.

A few years later Andy gave me that cross for my birthday, and it now hangs in our living room. Every time I look at it, I think of the Spirit that moved Andy to give a year of his life to helping young people, the Spirit that also moved him to make a cross to honor the memory of a young man who never had a chance to make something of his life.

Most readers probably do not pay much attention to the end of Luke's account of Peter's meeting with Cornelius: "Then they invited him to stay for several days" (10:48). What could be significant about that? It seems natural that the newly baptized Cornelius would want his new Christian teacher, who had known Jesus personally, to stay around to answer a few follow-up questions. Peter would most likely have been glad to spend some time with his newly baptized friend. But, in fact, a house visit was far from natural under the circumstances. And when Peter gets back to Jerusalem, he is criticized not because he baptized Cornelius but because he stayed at Cornelius's house.

Remember Peter's own words: "It is unlawful for a Jew to associate with or to visit a Gentile" (10:28). According to the way most Jews interpreted the Mosaic law, Gentiles' homes and the food they ate were considered ritually impure. Thus when Peter returns to Jerusalem, some in the Church criticize him: "Why did you go to uncircumcised men and eat with them?" (11:3).

Peter defends his actions by describing the series of events, beginning with his vision of pure and impure animals and ending with the "second Pentecost" at Cornelius's house (11:4–17). Peter succeeds in bringing the Jerusalem Christians to recognize that God has decided to invite non-Jews as well as Jews to faith in Jesus.

The Jerusalem Christians grant that Peter has been following the Spirit's initiative, but they now have to think through the implications of what God is doing. Through Baptism, Gentiles are both joined to Christ and incorporated into his body, the Church. The members of the Church are brothers and sisters in Christ; they share meals in each other's homes and care for each other's material needs. By accepting Cornelius's hospitality, Peter began to relate to the Gentile believers in just this way, as brothers and sisters in Christ. But how can Jewish Christians, who follow the Mosaic law, have such a close relationship with Gentile Christians, whose non-Jewish lifestyle makes them ritually impure?

In Peter's day, there were some Jewish Christians who thought they had a solution to the problem of remaining faithful Jews while being open to what God is doing with the Gentiles. These Jewish Christians thought that Gentile Christians should complete their conversion to the Jewish Messiah by becoming Jews. The men should be circumcised; men and women should agree to follow the Mosaic law. Then the Gentiles' salvation would be complete, and Jewish believers would be able to share their community life with them. Other Jewish Christians, however, were opposed to this solution.

This conflict will come to a head in our next reading. The events that will bring about the crisis are underway even as Peter speaks in Jerusalem. Jewish Christians, many of them Greek-speaking, have traveled from Jerusalem to Antioch (one of the largest cities of the Roman Empire, in present-day south-central Turkey). There they are preaching the gospel to Greek-speaking Gentiles with remarkable results. "The hand of the Lord was with them, and a great number became believers and turned to the Lord" (11:21). Antioch becomes Cornelius's house on a grand scale.

The Jerusalem Christians welcome these new Gentile converts in Antioch, even though their presence presents a theological and pastoral dilemma. The Christians are trying to follow the Spirit's initiative, even when they do not entirely understand where he is leading them. The Jerusalem church sends Barnabas as its representative to Antioch. He is pleased, and seems to be overwhelmed by the number of new Christians there. Barnabas goes to look for Paul and brings him to Antioch to share in the leadership.

Chapter 12 is about the murder of the apostle James, further persecution of Peter, and the death of Herod Agrippa. In chapters 13 and 14 Luke recounts how the Antioch church sends Barnabas and Paul out to evangelize on the island of Cyprus and in the region that is now central Turkey. Large numbers of Gentiles pour into the Church. The brewing crisis boils over.

5

Trying to Grasp What God Is Doing

Warm-Up Questions

1 Whose advice do you like to seek on important matters in your life? How does the advice of that person (or those persons) help you?

2 Which of the following statements comes closest to describing your approach to disagreements?
- ○ I close my eyes and hope they go away.
- ○ I assume that I must be wrong.
- ○ I always try to avoid confrontation.
- ○ I negotiate, compromise, and try to reach a rational conclusion.
- ○ I don't address the issue directly, but make little cutting remarks to let people know where I stand.
- ○ I don't put up a fight, but then play the martyr.
- ○ I manipulate situations behind the scenes.
- ○ I concentrate on winning at all costs.
- ○ I find that sometimes a good fight clears the air.

Opening the Bible

What's Happened

Now that Peter has brought the gospel to non-Jews, other Christians do the same on a larger scale. The church in Antioch proves to be very mission-minded. The Christians there send Barnabas and Paul to spread the word about Jesus to both Jews and Gentiles in present-day Cyprus and central Turkey. Like Cornelius, the Gentiles join the Church without becoming Jews. But once the Gentiles are baptized, should they begin following the Mosaic law? On this question there are sharply different views.

THE READING

Acts 15:1–35

Must Gentile Believers Become Jews?

15:1 Then certain individuals came down from Judea and were teaching the brothers, "Unless you are circumcised according to the custom of Moses, you cannot be saved." 2 And after Paul and Barnabas had no small dissension and debate with them, Paul and Barnabas and some of the others were appointed to go up to Jerusalem to discuss this question with the apostles and the elders. 3 So they were sent on their way by the church, and as they passed through both Phoenicia and Samaria, they reported the conversion of the Gentiles, and brought great joy to all the believers. 4 When they came to Jerusalem, they were welcomed by the church and the apostles and the elders, and they reported all that God had done with them. 5 But some believers who belonged to the sect of the Pharisees stood up and said, "It is necessary for them to be circumcised and ordered to keep the law of Moses."

6 The apostles and the elders met together to consider this matter. 7 After there had been much debate, Peter stood up and said to them, "My brothers, you know that in the early days God made a choice among you, that I should be the one through whom the Gentiles would hear the message of the good news and become believers. 8 And God, who knows the human heart, testified to them by giving them the Holy Spirit, just as he did to us; 9 and in cleansing their hearts by faith he has made no

distinction between them and us. [10] Now therefore why are you putting God to the test by placing on the neck of the disciples a yoke that neither our ancestors nor we have been able to bear? [11] On the contrary, we believe that we will be saved through the grace of the Lord Jesus, just as they will."

[12] The whole assembly kept silence, and listened to Barnabas and Paul as they told of all the signs and wonders that God had done through them among the Gentiles. [13] After they finished speaking, James replied, "My brothers, listen to me. [14] Simeon has related how God first looked favorably on the Gentiles, to take from among them a people for his name. [15] This agrees with the words of the prophets, as it is written,

[16] 'After this I will return,
and I will rebuild the dwelling of David, which has fallen;
   from its ruins I will rebuild it,
      and I will set it up,
[17] so that all other peoples may seek the Lord—
   even all the Gentiles over whom my name has been
      called.
   Thus says the Lord, who has been making these
      things [18] known from long ago.'

[19] Therefore I have reached the decision that we should not trouble those Gentiles who are turning to God, [20] but we should write to them to abstain only from things polluted by idols and from fornication and from whatever has been strangled and from blood. . . . "

[22] Then the apostles and the elders, with the consent of the whole church, decided to choose men from among their members and to send them to Antioch with Paul and Barnabas. They sent Judas called Barsabbas, and Silas, leaders among the brothers, [23] with the . . . letter. . . .

[30] So they were sent off and went down to Antioch. When they gathered the congregation together, they delivered the letter. [31] When its members read it, they rejoiced at the exhortation. [32] Judas and Silas, who were themselves prophets, said much to encourage and strengthen the believers. [33] After they had been there for some time, they were sent off in peace by the believers to those who had sent them. [35] But Paul and Barnabas remained in Antioch, and there, with many others, they taught and proclaimed the word of the Lord.

Questions for a Closer Look

1 Why would the Christians in Antioch send representatives to the Church in Jerusalem to resolve the issue that had arisen (15:1–2)?

2 What picture does this reading paint of the relationships between Christians in different localities in the early years of the Church?

3 On what kinds of evidence and what sorts of arguments do the apostles and elders base their decision?

4 What did each of the following men contribute to the discussion: Peter? Paul and Barnabas? James?

5 How did these early Christians go about resolving their disagreement? What lessons could be drawn from this for how disagreements might be handled in your family or at your school?

A Guide to the Reading

15:1 ~ In Cornelius's conversion, the Holy Spirit worked overtime to reveal God's will. Peter felt compelled to welcome Cornelius and his friends into the Church without circumcision, since God had already welcomed them into Christ without waiting for them to become Jews. But no matter how obvious the Spirit's activity, the Christians still had to deal with the question of whether the Baptism of Cornelius and company was to be considered the rule or an exception. Did it indicate the pattern the Church should now follow, or was it just an exception to the rule?

The question of admitting Gentiles into the Church without requiring them to become Jews raised serious issues. If Gentiles are saved by belief in Jesus without keeping the Mosaic law, then Jesus plays the central role in our relationship with God and not the Mosaic law. The Mosaic law erected a wall of ritual purity around those who observed it by defining certain foods, persons, and things as unclean. If Jesus, rather than the Mosaic law, is central in the Church, then Jesus does away with the separation that is based on ritual regulations.

To many Jewish Christians, this was unthinkable. They saw the Mosaic law as central, and insisted that Gentile converts follow it. Although Luke does not say so, these Jewish Christians probably refused to associate with the Gentile converts, considering them ritually impure.

15:2–4 ~ The Antioch community is large and mature enough to be sending out its own missionaries. Nevertheless, the Antioch Christians recognize the mother church in Jerusalem, headed by the apostles, as the central authority for resolving the disagreement. In Jerusalem, "elders" now share in leadership with the apostles. Luke implies that an orderly transfer of authority is underway from the apostles to the next generation of leaders.

15:5 ~ Some Jerusalem Christians who are Pharisees repeat the demand that the Gentile believers become Jews. The fact that Pharisees, who advocated scrupulous observance of the Mosaic law, were attracted to the Christian movement shows that in general the Jerusalem Christians kept the law carefully.

15:6–11 ~ Paul and Barnabas's missionary report is inspiring but it needs further development, which Peter attempts to supply. He tells the story of what happened at Cornelius's house. His concluding remark shows that he now understands that Jesus, not the Mosaic law, is the decisive factor in believers' relationship with God. Thus to insist that Gentile believers keep the Mosaic law would ignore what God has done through Jesus and the Spirit.

15:12 ~ The assembly shows that it agrees with Peter when it receives his argument with silence. But someone still needs to show how God's present action among the Gentiles connects with what God has already revealed. This is the task of James, a relative of Jesus, who is now the local leader of the Jerusalem community.

15:13–21 ~ James uses Scripture to show that what Peter has described fulfills God's long-standing intentions. Consequently, James says, Gentile converts should not be required to follow the Mosaic law. But what exactly should they be required to do? It is not clear what the prohibitions in verse 20 mean. There are two main possibilities. One is that James wants the Gentile believers to avoid eating nonkosher meat and to refrain from marrying close relatives so that Jewish believers can feel comfortable associating with them. The other is that he wants them to stay away from taking part in the worship of idols.

15:22–35 ~ The leaders and the rest of the Church accept James's decision. Jesus, rather than the Mosaic covenant, will be at the center of the Church. Israel's traditional focus on chosen land, temple, law, and national life will be left behind. The Church, centered on Jesus, will bring the gospel to people in *every* land; it will worship God through Jesus and the Spirit equally in *every* place; it will seek a deeper relationship with God not through observance of law but by personal discipleship to Jesus. It will be a community open to every people and every culture.

Questions for Application

1 Paul, Barnabas, and Peter were attentive to what the Spirit was doing. How can we tell where God is at work in our lives and in the world around us? What is the value of talking with others about what we think God is doing?

2 What does it mean to have Jesus at the center of your life? What competes with Jesus for center stage in your life? What could we do to keep our lives better focused on Jesus?

3 What is a lesson we can learn from how the early Christians resolve their disagreement in this chapter?

4 What are some of the things that keep your school from being the best possible Christian community? What could you do to help your school become a better Christian community?

5 When you have to make an important decision, whom do you consult? What qualities do you look for in someone whose advice you seek?

6 Describe an experience which helped you to listen carefully to another person. How did this experience affect you?

Approach to Prayer

Pray the Hail Mary together with the group to begin. Then take a few moments for silent reflection, asking God for wisdom to deal with problems in your personal life, in your home, in your school, and among your friends. Then pray together with the group this prayer, which some Byzantine Catholics pray in the liturgy between the Scripture readings and the homily.

> *Heavenly king, Comforter, Spirit*
> *of truth, you are present everywhere*
> *and fill all things. Treasury of*
> *blessings and giver of life, come*
> *and dwell within us, cleanse us*
> *of all stain, and save our*
> *souls, O gracious Lord.*

Saints in the Making

A Constructive Approach to Controversy

Those who conducted the council in Jerusalem left future generations of Christians a model for handling disagreement. An early observer to remark on this model was Saint John Chrysostom. In the summer of 400, Bishop John preached several homilies on Acts 15 to his congregation in Constantinople, which is now called Istanbul. Perhaps the many disputes that troubled the Church of his day helped him appreciate the importance of constructive conflict resolution.

John pointed out that in Acts the church leaders did not look for someone on whom to blame everything. The Jewish Christians who had gone to Antioch insisting that Gentile converts be circumcised had not been authorized by the Jerusalem church leadership, so there were grounds for making accusations against them. Paul and Barnabas, however, "do not show up making accusations, but 'declaring all the things that God had done with them,'" John observed. The Jerusalem leaders, who could have focused on the self-appointed teachers' insubordination, spoke "mildly," John said, "and not with an emphasis on their authority. Such amiable words are more likely to fix themselves in the mind. . . . Notice how they say nothing harsh against the unauthorized teachers but focus on undoing the damage that has been done. . . . They do not call them, 'Seducers!' or 'Pestilent fellows!' or anything like that."

Indeed, John remarked, gentleness characterized the church leaders' entire handling of the disagreement. This was best, John said, for "gentleness is everywhere a great good, while it is impossible for one who is out of temper ever to persuade." The leaders did not throw their weight around, John noted. After Peter spoke, "The entire assembly kept silence. There was no arrogance in the church." While Peter and Paul spoke, no one interrupted;

and James, who was in charge, waited patiently. "The orderliness was great because their hearts were free from love of glory!"

Finally, John thought the council was wise to involve both those who were engaged in the controversial activities (Peter, Paul, and Barnabas, who had preached to Gentiles) and someone who was uninvolved (James). James was able to argue dispassionately, without having to worry about defending his actions.

John's commentary helps us appreciate how relevant the story is to young people as they face situations of disagreement with their parents, their teachers, and even their friends. There needs to be more than good intentions in settling disputes: there must also be patience, gentleness, workable strategies, and effective use of mediators.

Between Discussions

Choosing six readings from Acts is a frustrating task because the selection inevitably will be unbalanced. The readings in this volume are concentrated in the first half of Acts. As a result the selection is heavy on the church in Jerusalem and light on the churches in the Gentile world.

Another imbalance concerns women. Both men and women have been present in many of the scenes so far—receiving the Spirit at Pentecost, listening to Peter's preaching in the Temple, embracing the gospel at Cornelius's house. But the individuals identified by name are almost all men.

In other sections of Acts, however, several women step out of the anonymous crowd and into the spotlight. Almost all of them play a constructive role in the early Church. These women do not give the great speeches or head the pioneer missionary teams. Luke shows them moving within the more ordinary range of Christians' activities of the time. Taking a look at these women, then, puts us in touch with important aspects of Christian life "on the ground," as most Christians experienced it. Here, briefly, are the more important of these women.

Mary (1:13–14) ~ The mother of Jesus is glimpsed sitting upstairs in a large house in Jerusalem among the followers of Jesus who are waiting for the Spirit. Her presence must have been an encouragement to trust in God, for she was a living witness to God's faithfulness to his promises. Mary's role in the Church was utterly unique: she was the mother of the Lord. Yet she was also a model disciple, for she exemplified how every disciple of the Lord ought to listen for his word, receive it with faith, and be totally available for his plans.

Tabitha (9:36–42) ~ She is a "female disciple." She devoted her time and money to caring for poor people, which shows that she had material means at her disposal. Tabitha responded to the gospel in a practical manner by using her resources to help others. But she did more than write checks; she gave of herself: the recipients of her generosity show Peter the clothing she made for them. Tabitha experienced God's action in a remarkable way, for after she died, Peter raised her back to life through prayer.

Mary, the mother of John Mark (12:12–17) ~ She too was a woman of means, for she had a home large enough to host meetings of Christians in Jerusalem. While her son John Mark and another relative, Barnabas, went on missionary journeys, Mary remained at home. But she was not cut off from the world. In those days a variety of activities took place in the homes of more affluent people: business was transacted; goods were made and sold; sick and needy persons were cared for; and relatives, friends, and clients interacted with one another. Mary may have played an important part in many people's lives, not least in the lives of the Christians who met regularly in her home.

Lydia (16:12–40) ~ We read about this businesswoman in Week 6.

Philip's daughters (21:9) ~ Like the martyred Stephen, Philip was one of the seven Greek-speaking Jewish leaders in Jerusalem. He left Jerusalem and spread the gospel in various places, ending up in Caesarea. His four daughters are mentioned only in passing, but what Luke says about them is significant. Philip's daughters exercised the gift of prophecy. Their role of delivering inspired messages from the Lord would have been greatly valued and may have had a significant effect on the Church.

Priscilla (18:1–3,18,24–26) ~ She and her husband, Aquila, shared their home and their work, making leather tents, with Paul. They also traveled with Paul. When a promising and well-educated Christian speaker named Apollos arrived in town needing more instruction in the faith, Paul turned him over to Priscilla and Aquila. Because Luke mentions Priscilla before Aquila, it would seem that she played at least an equal part in Apollos's further education. Since Apollos had already obtained an excellent literary and religious education, we can only conclude that Priscilla and her husband were highly educated and reliable Christian teachers.

Missionary Adventures

Warm-Up Questions

1 Have you ever made a hasty judgment about someone and later realized you were mistaken? What did you learn from this mistake?

2 When do you sing?
- ○ When I'm happy
- ○ When I'm depressed, to keep my spirits up
- ○ Only when I'm alone (in my room or in the shower)
- ○ As much as possible
- ○ On certain occasions when I'm with certain other people
- ○ Only when I'm at church
- ○ Never

Opening the Bible

Acts 15:36–40; 16:8–40

A Missionary Journey

[15:36] After some days Paul said to Barnabas, "Come, let us return and visit the believers in every city where we proclaimed the word of the Lord and see how they are doing." [37] Barnabas wanted to take with them John called Mark. [38] But Paul decided not to take with them one who had deserted them in Pamphylia and had not accompanied them in the work. [39] The disagreement became so sharp that they parted company; Barnabas took Mark with him and sailed away to Cyprus. [40] But Paul chose Silas and set out, the believers commending him to the grace of the Lord. . . .

[16:8] [P]assing by Mysia, they went down to Troas. [9] During the night Paul had a vision: there stood a man of Macedonia pleading with him and saying, "Come over to Macedonia and help us." [10] When he had seen the vision, we immediately tried to cross over to Macedonia, being convinced that God had called us to proclaim the good news to them.

[11] We set sail from Troas and took a straight course to Samothrace, the following day to Neapolis, [12] and from there to Philippi, which is a leading city of the district of Macedonia and a Roman colony. . . . [13] On the sabbath day we went outside the gate by the river, where we supposed there was a place of prayer; and we sat down and spoke to the women who had gathered there. [14] A certain woman named Lydia, a worshiper of God, was listening to us; she was from the city of Thyatira and a dealer in purple cloth. The Lord opened her heart to listen eagerly to what was said by Paul. [15] When she and her household were baptized, she urged us, saying, "If you have judged me to be faithful to the Lord, come and stay at my home." And she prevailed upon us.

The Downs and Ups of Christian Mission

[16] One day, as we were going to the place of prayer, we met a slave-girl who had a spirit of divination and brought her owners a great deal of money by fortune telling. [17] While she followed Paul and us, she would cry out, "These men are slaves of the Most High

God, who proclaim to you a way of salvation." [18] ... But Paul, very much annoyed, turned and said to the spirit, "I order you in the name of Jesus Christ to come out of her." And it came out that very hour.

[19] But when her owners saw that their hope of making money was gone, they seized Paul and Silas and dragged them into the marketplace before the authorities. [20] When they had brought them before the magistrates, they said, "These men are disturbing our city; they are Jews [21] and are advocating customs that are not lawful for us as Romans to adopt or observe." [22] The crowd joined in attacking them, and the magistrates had them stripped of their clothing and ordered them to be beaten with rods. [23] After they had given them a severe flogging, they threw them into prison. . . .

[25] About midnight Paul and Silas were praying and singing hymns to God, and the prisoners were listening to them. [26] Suddenly there was an earthquake, so violent that the foundations of the prison were shaken; and immediately all the doors were opened and everyone's chains were unfastened. [27] When the jailer woke up and saw the prison doors wide open, he drew his sword and was about to kill himself, since he supposed that the prisoners had escaped. [28] But Paul shouted in a loud voice, "Do not harm yourself, for we are all here." [29] The jailer called for lights, and rushing in, he fell down trembling before Paul and Silas. [30] Then he brought them outside and said, "Sirs, what must I do to be saved?" [31] They answered, "Believe on the Lord Jesus, and you will be saved, you and your household." [32] They spoke the word of the Lord to him and to all who were in his house. [33] At the same hour of the night he took them and washed their wounds; then he and his entire family were baptized without delay. [34] He brought them up into the house and set food before them; and he and his entire household rejoiced that he had become a believer in God.

[35] When morning came, the magistrates sent the police, saying, "Let those men go." . . . [37] But Paul replied, "They have beaten us in public, uncondemned, men who are Roman citizens, and have thrown us into prison; and now are they going to discharge us in secret? Certainly not! Let them come and take us out themselves." [38] The police reported these words to the magistrates, and they were afraid when they heard that they were Roman citizens; [39] so they came and apologized to them. And they took them out and asked them to leave the city. [40] After leaving the prison they went to Lydia's home; and when they had seen and encouraged the brothers and sisters there, they departed.

Questions for a Closer Look

1 Philippi is a Roman settlement. How does Roman law work for and against the Christians in this week's reading?

2 Luke says that the Spirit guided Lydia to listen carefully to Paul. In what way was God involved in preparing the jailer to be receptive to Paul's message?

3 What does the location of the Jewish place of prayer (16:13) suggest about the place that Jews occupied in Philippian society? What do verses 20–23 add to the picture of Jews in the city? In light of this, how easy would it have been for the jailer and his household, who were not Jews, to embrace the message of the Jewish–Christian missionaries?

4 At what point does Luke begin using "we" and "us"? Where does he seem to be at the beginning of this reading? Where is he at the end?

5 What does this reading tell you about the kind of person Paul was? How is this picture affected by considering also what is said about him in the readings in Weeks 3 and 5?

A Guide to the Reading

15:36–40 ~ Following the agreement on the issue of the Gentiles, a disagreement takes place between Barnabas and Paul. They are planning to visit some places where they had preached the gospel, and they cannot agree on whether or not to take along John Mark. Paul refuses to take him because John Mark had abandoned them halfway into their last trip. He seems concerned that John Mark will leave them again at some dangerous moment. Barnabas seems willing to overlook the risk, possibly because John Mark is his cousin.

Barnabas and Paul are unable to resolve their disagreement, so they separate. This is the last mention of Barnabas in Acts. Does this mean that family loyalties were more important to him than the missionary work he was doing? Or is it a sign that Paul was unbending and domineering? Luke does not answer these questions, and we are left wondering about the interplay of God's Spirit and human personalities. The Church is indeed a mysterious combination of divine and (flawed) human elements. (In his letter to Philemon, Paul seems to suggest that he and John Mark were later reconciled.)

16:8–12 ~ Paul and Silas travel west through what is now Turkey. When they arrive at the coast, a dream guides them to sail to a region within present-day Greece. Notice the "we" in verse 10. Apparently Luke has joined the missionary team.

16:13–15 ~ Philippi was a town with mostly Roman immigrants; there were few Jewish residents and no synagogue. It is not clear whether the "place of prayer" was a building for Jewish meetings outside the city or simply an outdoor area for gathering. At the place of prayer, Paul and his friends run into some women, one of whom is Lydia, a well-to-do merchant of dyed fabrics. Luke's statement that "the Lord opened her heart to listen eagerly" nicely balances the action of the Spirit and Lydia's response. The Spirit inspires her to pay attention but does not force her to believe in Jesus; yet she could not believe without the Spirit's help.

16:16–18 ~ The fortune teller's proclamation that the missionaries represent the "Most High God" and teach a way of "salvation" might seem like a welcome confirmation. But listeners could have misunderstood it to mean that the men were agents of *Zeus* bringing *magical healing.*

16:19–24 ~ There was much anti-Jewish feeling in ancient Mediterranean cities, so it was not hard to stir up a crowd against Jews. To soothe the crowd, the judges have the out-of-town troublemakers beaten and jailed without bothering to investigate.

16:25–26 ~ Acts contains many descriptions of the Spirit's effects on those who believe in Jesus. Perhaps the most remarkable effects are the Christians' responses to suffering. The imprisoned missionaries' joyful praise of God seems a more powerful manifestation of the Spirit than the earthquake that breaks open the jail.

16:27–34 ~ The jailer may regard Paul and Silas as magicians whose prayers have caused the earthquake. His question in 16:30 may mean, "What can I do to keep you from getting angry?" Paul and Silas are always anxious to present the gospel, so they tell him about Jesus. The jailer is converted on the spot. Before bringing Paul and Silas into his house, he washes their wounds, and he and his household are baptized.

16:35–39 ~ In Roman settlements such as Philippi, the judges had only limited authority to imprison or physically punish Roman citizens. Why don't Paul and Silas declare their citizenship *before* getting beaten? It is likely that not all the members of the new Christian community are protected by Roman citizenship. Paul might feel that he can hardly encourage them to accept suffering for Christ if he uses his privileges to escape persecution. A concern for the converts might also explain why Paul insists that the judges admit their mistake. If the judges are publicly shamed for their attack on the missionaries, they might be inclined to leave the other Christians alone.

16:40 ~ Lydia's house has become the meeting place and center of the Philippian church, a crucial service for a community that has no legal recognition or church building.

Questions for Application

1 Paul had a vision about going to Macedonia. Do you think that God gives you signs telling you what he wants you to do in life? Has something ever happened to you that seemed more than a coincidence?

2 For some people, disagreements within the Church are an obstacle to believing that the Church is the Body of Christ. Do you feel this way? How can settling disputes actually help a community become closer?

3 The gospel came to Lydia and the jailer in different ways, one in an ordinary way, the other in an extraordinary way. In what ordinary ways has the gospel come to you? Has anything extraordinary happened to you that helped you get closer to God?

4 The girl's prophetic announcement in 16:17 was open to misunderstanding. What aspects of the Christian message are open to misunderstandings today?

5 How would you feel if you were trying to be of service to someone and you were treated unfairly? What do you think of the response of Paul and Silas in 16:25?

Approach to Prayer

Listen as a member of the group reads the following petitions aloud. After each petition, respond with "Empower us by your Spirit, O Lord."

So that we might be love-bearers and peacemakers in our homes...

So that we might learn as students the lessons that will carry us through life...

So that we might be messengers of God's Word to those around us...

So that we might work to make the world a better place...

So that we might find fulfillment in leading good lives...

End by praying the Our Father aloud with the group.

Saints in the Making

Grace at Pentecost

Louise de Marillac's husband was ill, and the couple faced financial difficulties. She was experiencing strong feelings of guilt and doubt because, even though she loved her husband, Antoine, she was afraid that she had offended God by marrying after first deciding to enter the convent. She wondered: Is there any life after death? Is there really a God?

People close to Louise gave her good advice. A bishop friend assured her that she would find peace. An uncle advised her to let go of her own plans for her life and to receive from God whatever he wished to give her. But at the feast of the Ascension in 1623, she was close to despair. None of her efforts, no prayer, seemed to help.

But then God spoke to her, 10 days later during Mass on Pentecost. He removed her sense of guilt about marrying and let her know that a new opportunity for religious life would open up. He also guided her to a new spiritual director. God's voice in her heart was very clear, and it overcame her doubts.

This Pentecost experience renewed Louise's relationship with God, but a painful period followed. Antoine died. Louise's financial problems worsened. Her situation as a widow, however, gave her a new freedom, and a priest named Vincent de Paul helped her figure out what God wanted her to do with it. Vincent was the leader of a movement to provide basic necessities to destitute people such as orphans and prisoners. Louise began to work with him.

Each year, Louise used the days from Ascension to Pentecost as a special time of retreat and prayer. The Pentecost season, filled with an awareness of the action of the Spirit, was always a particularly happy and fruitful time for her.

For more than 30 years Louise and Vincent cooperated in organizing a growing number of French women and men for service to the poor. Their slogan was "The poor are Jesus Christ." Vincent and Louise's efforts to care for the neediest people continue today through the religious orders they founded, the Vincentians and the Sisters of Charity, and the St. Vincent de Paul Society, an association of laypeople. Louise was canonized in 1934, and she is considered the patron saint of social workers.

Today, many parish youth groups, CCD programs, and Catholic schools encourage young people to get involved in working with the poor. These groups help young Catholics learn what Louise learned through her Pentecost experience—that "the poor are Jesus Christ."

After Words

After the episode at Philippi, the rest of Acts focuses on Paul. Luke tells us about the growth of the Church not by giving us a list of cities to which Christianity spread and figures on the number of people who were baptized but by following Paul's travels and church-founding, his arrest, imprisonment, shipwreck, and continued preaching. Luke's way of recording the Church's early history reminds us that ultimately it is not programs or institutions that communicate the Gospel, but men and women.

Chapters 17–20 ~ Paul and his companions travel from Philippi through present-day Greece and western Turkey. In each city Paul preaches in the synagogue, where he has a chance to speak about Messiah Jesus to Jews as well as to Gentiles who are admirers of Judaism. In city after city some Jews and "God-fearing" Gentiles accept the gospel, but sooner or later other Jews gang up on Paul and drive him out of town.

Paul preaches even to Gentiles who have no connection with Judaism. This brings some men and women to faith in Christ, but it also lands Paul in deep trouble with the people who believe in pagan gods and goddesses. In Ephesus, Paul's activities spark a massive riot by people who earn a living from the pilgrims who visit the immense shrine to the goddess Artemis. The people are afraid that conversions to Christianity will cut into their business.

As the Christian community grows away from its origins in Judaism, Christian missionaries spend less time trying to convince Jews that Jesus is the Messiah. They learn from Paul's experience and begin to spend more time persuading the Gentile worshipers of pagan gods that there is really only one God and Jesus is his Son. Persecution by Jewish authorities will become less of a problem as Christians address themselves more and more to Gentiles. Meanwhile, organized repression from the pagan Roman government will grow, leading eventually to systematic persecutions in the third and early fourth centuries.

Chapters 21–22 ~ Paul turns east and would like to celebrate Pentecost in Jerusalem. He visits groups of disciples in different cities along the way, and some Christians are inspired by the Spirit to warn him that danger awaits him in the holy city. Sure enough, a misunderstanding occurs when Paul gets to Jerusalem and a riot breaks out in the Temple. Paul is about to be killed when the Roman military intervenes and puts him in protective custody.

Chapters 23–28 ~ Paul is under arrest for the remainder of Acts. He is questioned in Jerusalem and at Caesarea, the Romans' provincial capital in Palestine. The Roman authorities do not wish to anger the Jewish leaders in Jerusalem, so they allow the case to drag on without resolution for a couple of years.

Paul is a Roman citizen and has the right to have the case transferred to a Roman court, and he finally exercises his right. The governor sends Paul under guard by sea to Rome. The ship is lost in a storm, and Paul and the other passengers barely survive. Luke's account is not only one of the greatest sea stories to come to us from the ancient world; it also lets us see Paul as a spiritual man who has a humane sense of solidarity with his guards and fellow passengers.

Acts ends on what may seem like a dissatisfying note. Paul is under house arrest in Rome. We are not told whether his case ever comes to trial or, if it does, what the outcome is. Is Paul released to continue his missionary work? Is he found guilty? If so, of what crime? With what punishment?

Not surprisingly, there has been a lot of debate about this ending. Some scholars wonder whether Luke's original conclusion has been lost. But others argue that this is indeed how Luke intended to bring his work to a close. Jesus had commissioned his followers to make him known from Jerusalem to the ends of the earth. In the final scene of Acts 28, Luke shows that the gospel has moved from Jerusalem to the center of the political and cultural world of the day. Now it is up to Luke's readers to carry out the rest of the commission and bring the gospel to the ends of the world.

You Shall Receive Power

The Main Character in Acts
Is Known Through His Impact on People

At the beginning of his public ministry, after being baptized by John the Baptist, Jesus returned to Galilee and began to announce that the Kingdom of God was about to arrive. People saw him as he walked along the lakeshore. They heard his voice. If they were near him in the synagogue on the Sabbath, they felt and smelled him. His disciples ate meals with him and slept in the same room with him at Peter's house in Capernaum. None of this was in the least remarkable. Jesus was "one in being with the Father," as we affirm in the creed, yet he was also a human being.

By contrast, when the Holy Spirit came to Jesus' disciples on Pentecost, they experienced wonderful things—a noise like wind, a brightness like fire—but they could neither see nor hear the Spirit himself. The Spirit did not have a body, as Jesus did, and thus could not be directly observed. He could be known only through the things he did.

In a sense, the Holy Spirit is the main character in Acts in the same way that Jesus is the main character in the Gospels. But we have to read Acts differently from the Gospels to follow the main character. In the Gospels the main character is before our eyes. In Acts, we must find the main character in his effects on people.

Fortunately this is not difficult to do. Luke has made the dots fairly prominent, and it is not too hard to connect them to form a sketch of the Spirit at work in the early Church. The early chapters of Acts are filled with signs of the Spirit that are easy to detect. Here are some of those signs. What others can you discover?

Peter became courageous. ~ Earlier, despite his best intentions, Peter had acted as a coward in denying that he knew Jesus. After the Spirit came, he spoke about Jesus publicly and boldly, without concern for his own safety (2:14; 4:8–20; 5:27–32,40–42).

People who had rejected Jesus accepted him. ~ When Peter spoke in the power of the Spirit, some of the very people who had demanded Jesus' execution came to believe that he is the Messiah (2:37–42; 3:13–17; 4:4).

The apostles understood how God is working in these "last days." ~ During his ministry, Jesus' closest followers had expected him to lead the national liberation of Israel. They had continued to nurse this hope even after he rose from the dead. With the coming of the Spirit, they understood that, instead of "restoring the kingdom to Israel," God is offering his Spirit to men and women to bring them into unity with himself and one another (2:38–39,43–47).

Jesus' disciples became united in love and service. ~ Once the Spirit came, Jesus' followers stopped arguing among themselves and developed into a community of people who cared for each other.

At this point, you may wish to pause and draw your own picture of the Holy Spirit. From the evidence of his actions in Acts, what kind of person do you conceive the Spirit to be? Luke's account suggests many lines of reflection on the Spirit. You might pay special attention to these characteristics of the Spirit:

1. The Spirit continues Jesus' work, with a multiplier effect. ~ Peter had been with Jesus day after day for months, even years, listening to his teaching and receiving his direction. Yet some weakness in him remained unchanged. It was the Spirit that empowered Peter to be the man Jesus called him to be.

Jesus had attracted crowds with his miracles and preaching. But the community of committed followers that he left behind was small: only 120 disciples were gathered in Jerusalem. By contrast, after Peter's Spirit-filled preaching on Pentecost, three thousand people committed their lives to Jesus.

Jesus had patiently taught his followers about the kingdom of mercy and humble service that he came to bring. But even the inner circle of his disciples did not grasp his message. No matter how many times he corrected them, they continued to look forward to occupying prominent positions when Jesus began to rule. The Spirit, however, changed these ambitious men into a group of servant-leaders, able to guide others in a community life marked by mutual love.

The point of these comparisons is not to diminish Jesus but to highlight the Spirit. The Spirit's action depended on what Jesus had accomplished. The Spirit came only after Jesus died and rose. Yet we cannot help but be impressed by how powerfully the Spirit built on Jesus' accomplishments. The Spirit completed things that Jesus had only begun. Jesus told the disciples that it was good for them that he was going away because only then would the Spirit come. Then they would do greater things than he had done.

Our own worries and distractions, our desire for comfortable routines, and our lack of faith may make us insensitive to the Spirit's presence. Our awareness of the Spirit may be faint. But we have cause to hope. The Spirit is among us today, just as he was among the first Christians. He can act powerfully to complete what Jesus has begun in our lives. Perhaps he is simply waiting for us to tell him that it's OK for him to shake up our lives, so that we too will experience the impact of his presence.

2. The Spirit turns each of us outward, to each other and to the world. ~ Like a magnet attracting pieces of metal, the Spirit draws us into serving one another and carrying out Christ's mission to the world.

Luke shows us that new believers became willing to look beyond their personal interests and to spend their time and money caring for those among them who were in need. Helping widows and orphans was not a way to move up in society or to make one's own life more comfortable; this was an expression of love.

The apostles were willing, even glad, to endure the beatings and imprisonments that came their way as they preached the gospel. Their willingness stemmed from their deep desire for men and women to experience God's grace through Jesus.

Self-interest still existed in the Christian community, as we see from the incident with Ananias and Sapphira, who tried to keep some of their property for themselves. Missionaries did not always get along with each other. But there was something powerful at work in the Christian community enabling the believers to overcome their tendency to look out for their own interests. This powerful agent was the Holy Spirit.

Luke does not explore the inner transformation that the Spirit accomplishes as he guides the soul on the journey toward God. That task would fall to later spiritual writers like Saint John of the Cross and Saint Teresa of Ávila. But Luke shows us the fundamental direction of the Spirit's action in us: outward, away from self, toward neighbor, and toward God. The Spirit puts us in touch with the needs of others and with the tempo of God's action. From the Spirit we receive the freedom to put our own interests second to the needs of other people. We are able to pray the Our Father with real longing: "May your kingdom come, may your will be done, on earth as in heaven."

This understanding of the Spirit's action gives us a vital clue on how to connect with his power. If we wish to experience the Spirit, we should become involved with what the Spirit is doing. Since the Spirit is making us a more loving community and helping us bring the light of Christ into the world, we can expect to experience the Spirit working in us as we try to serve within the Church and take part in the Church's mission. In other words, the more we bring our lives into line with what the Spirit is doing, the more we will experience his gifts and graces.

Perhaps Peter discovered his new boldness only when he stood up to speak to the crowd on Pentecost morning. Perhaps some of the Christians in Jerusalem realized how greatly they loved one another only when they sold their property and brought the proceeds to the apostles for distribution to the needy brothers and sisters. Perhaps Paul discovered how deeply he wanted God's Kingdom to come only on the night when he sat in a dark jail in Philippi and found himself singing praises to God.

If we start moving in the direction in which the Spirit wants us to move, we can be sure that we will experience his power helping us along the way.

Other Ways of Saying *Church*

I n Acts, Luke often writes about the Church without using the Greek word for *church*. Instead he uses descriptive terms, such as "the whole group of those who believed" and "the whole community of the disciples." These different ways of speaking about the Church give us much to think about our identity today as Jesus' followers. Below are some of the descriptions Luke uses for the Church and ideas on how these words apply to us today.

1. "My witnesses" ~ Before Pentecost, Jesus tells his followers that when the Spirit comes, "You will be my witnesses in Jerusalem, in all Judea and Samaria, and to the ends of the earth"(1:8). This statement sets the agenda for Acts, which tells the story of the Church's growth from a small gathering of Jewish men and women in a house in Jerusalem to a network of Jewish-Gentile communities spread across the Roman empire.

Jesus' words set an agenda for our lives too. "You shall be my witnesses." His words force us to ask ourselves how well our lives reflect him to other people. Do people experience his humility and compassion when they come in contact with us? What is there about our lives that might lead others to conclude that we are believers in the risen Lord? Do we make our faith in Jesus clear to others so that they have a chance to come to know him?

2. "The disciples" ~ Luke speaks often of the "community of the disciples" and more often simply of "the disciples." More than mere students, disciples have a close relationship with their master. To call the Christian movement a community of disciples means that it is composed of men and women, each of whom has a one-on-one relationship with Jesus. Furthermore, disciples are not just companions; they are learners. The Church, then, is a community of learners. No one can be perfect, but neither is anyone free to drift along without learning and changing. Each of us is on a program of change with the help of our personal trainer, Jesus. Do you think of yourself as a disciple of Jesus?

3. Those who "belonged to the Way" (9:2) ~ This suggests that the Church is on a road to God, and that its members follow a way of life together. What does it mean to think of your life as a pilgrimage toward God? What aspect of your life is Jesus calling you to reshape to fit his way of living?

4. "Brothers and sisters" ~ Luke often refers to groups of Christians as "brothers" (for example, 10:23), and Christians often address each other as "brothers" (9:17; 15:7,13).

In ancient times the family was the glue that held life together. There were no government programs to help people, so people depended on their relatives. To call someone your brother or sister was to recognize a commitment. Jesus called his followers to commit their whole lives to him; this, in turn, meant that they had a relationship with one another. Jesus described the result in terms of family: "Looking at those who sat around him, he said, 'Here are my mother and my brothers! Whoever does the will of God is my brother and sister and mother'" (Mark 3:34–35).

After Pentecost Jesus' followers continued to recognize each other as brothers and sisters. They created smaller groupings of fellow disciples, such as home-based groupings, and they established distinct sections of the community for different language groups. These smaller groupings enabled the followers to maintain a familial relationship with each other, even as the community grew to thousands of members.

Have you experienced in your local church family (your youth group or CCD program or Catholic school) the kind of affection, trust, care, and commitment to each other that one would expect to find in a family? Would developing smaller groupings within the Church to enable members to know and care for each other helpful?

5. The "fellowship" (2:42) ~ The Greek word for "fellowship" suggests a form of life that is communal. It means sharing or participating in something together. The Christians shared in the apostles' message about Jesus and in the Spirit, and that sharing brought about a fellowship, or community, with one another.

6. Those who "had all things in common" (2:44) ~ Because they shared in the life of God together, the believers also shared their material resources with each other.

Luke does not give us details on how exactly the Christians in Jerusalem did this. Apparently the sharing was voluntary. The sharing may have involved eating daily meals together, rather than simply a distribution of funds. In other words, the material sharing involved a real sharing of life. Wealthier and poorer members of the community were drawn into a relationship with each other that they would not have had without the community.

This example spurs us to examine our own situations and evaluate the care that we offer one another. Many youth groups and religion classes are involved in service to needy people in their communities. Have you participated in such efforts? What efforts could you make so that in your community the words, "There was not a needy person among them" (4:34) would be fulfilled? What experience have you had of wealthier and poorer Christians treating each other as brothers and sisters? Have you ever known them to share meals together?

7. The renewed community of Israel ~ Luke does not use this term, but it is present in his mind and in the minds of the apostles, as we can see from an incident after Jesus' ascension (1:15–26). Jesus had chosen 12 of his disciples to function as an inner group. One of the disciples, Judas, abandoned his place by betraying Jesus. While Jesus' followers waited for the Spirit, Peter guided them in choosing a replacement for Judas. Peter thought it was important for the group of 12 to be at full strength for launching the Church because that number helped express what the Church is. Twelve was the number of tribes that traditionally constituted Israel. Thus the 12 apostles symbolized that the community of Jesus' followers was the renewed people of Israel gathered around Israel's Messiah.

The Church began not as a replacement of Israel, let alone a separate religion, but as the renewal of Israel. Since those early days, Christianity and Judaism have gone separate ways, sometimes with animosity. But in the Church, which believes that its Lord is the Jewish Messiah, there is absolutely no place for prejudice toward Jews and Judaism. The Second Vatican Council says that "the church . . . mindful of her common patrimony with the Jews . . . deplores . . . . anti-Semitism directed against the Jews at any time and from any source" (*Declaration on the Relationship of the Church to Non-Christian Religions,* section 4). It is true that the gospel encountered opposition in first-century Judaism. But to the Jewish Christians like Peter and John who faced this opposition, the idea of "Christian anti-Semitism" would have seemed an absurd self-contradiction.

8. "Me" (9:4,16) ~ Speaking to Paul, Jesus refers to the members of the Church who are suffering persecution for him as parts of himself: "Why do you persecute *me?*" (italics added). The members of the Church are joined to Christ like hands are joined to the body. Jesus in heaven is profoundly united with his followers on earth.

This unity has many implications. Jesus' words in Acts 9:16 specifically concern the sharing of suffering between himself and his followers. His words suggest that we might call the Church "the community of those who share in Jesus' suffering."

Are you and I willing to offer our sufferings to God, in union with Jesus, for the advancement of his kingdom in the world? Will we share in the Church's work in the world, even when it becomes difficult and painful? As fellow members of the Body of Christ, let us pray for each other that our answer will be yes.

Listening When God Speaks

As you have worked your way through this book, you have been listening to God's word. But this is not the first time that God has spoken to you, and indeed God has been speaking to you throughout your young life. Let's look at some of the ways that God speaks to you, and how you can improve your listening skills.

The most obvious way that you receive messages from God is through the Scripture, which is the Word of God. The people of Israel and the early Christians recorded their experiences of God's saving acts in history, and our religious tradition accepts their writings as God's Word to us. We believe that when we read Scripture, or hear it read, God is communicating his Word to us. It would be a good thing for you to develop the habit of reading the Bible on a regular basis, and you should make every effort to benefit from the weekly reading of Scripture at Mass.

An excellent way in which to listen to God speaking to us in Scripture is to pray the Scripture. Begin by adopting a proper prayer *posture* through the selection of an appropriate time and place for prayer. Once in the proper posture, become aware of God's *presence* in your life and in the time and place you have chosen for your prayer. Then *pray* for guidance from the Holy Spirit, asking help to understand the passage on which you will be reading and reflecting. You are now ready to read your selected *passage,* but you must read slowly and deliberately, with the intention of hearing God's voice in the passage. After you have read and reread the passage, *pause* for reflection on the passage. Allow time for God to speak to you through the words of the text.

The Bible is the Word of God, but it is not the only Word of God. Jesus Christ is also the Word of God, the Word made flesh. The Gospel of John begins with that message: "In the beginning was the Word, and the Word was with God, and the Word was God. . . . And the Word became flesh and made his dwelling among us." We want, then, to listen to God speaking to us in Jesus Christ and one good way to do that is by participating fully in Mass. Gathering together with the other worshipers, we enter into communion with them and with the presiding priest. The words and actions of the celebration put our spirits at rest, so that by the time we enter into communion with Christ in the Eucharist, we are in a position to hear God's message of love, peace, and salvation. We should not make the mistake of thinking that Jesus speaks to us only at the moment of receiving the Eucharist. His voice can be heard—if only we listen—through the community, through the priest, through the entire Eucharistic celebration, and finally, bringing it all together, in the eating and drinking of the Body and Blood of Christ.

Because the Church is the Body of Christ, we can also speak of the Church as the Word of God. God speaks to us through the community of believers, and in a special way through the leadership of that community. One way to listen to the voice of God in the Church is by paying attention to the voices of the believers nearest us: our parents and teachers, our parish priest, and the people with whom we worship on Sunday. Another way is to stay in touch with what the leadership of our Church is teaching. The bishops of our Church, especially the bishop of Rome, the Holy Father, and our own local bishop, the leader of the Church where we are active, speak to us in words that have the authority of the Word of God, and as Catholics we hear in them the voice of God.

Finally, God speaks to us in our own life experiences. The Second Vatican Council recovered the biblical image of "reading the signs of the times," that is, hearing the voice of God in the events of history. On the personal level, we can hear God speaking to us in such things as our encounters with others, our decisions, our successes and failures, and the challenges arising from the difficulties of life. To hear God's voice in our life experiences, we need to pay attention to those experiences, reflect on them, and learn from them.

There is a wonderful story in the Old Testament about a young boy named Samuel. (1 Samuel 3.) Samuel was assisting an old priest named Eli, who was waiting in the Temple for God to speak to him. One night while he was sleeping, Samuel heard someone call him. He assumed it was Eli, so he went and woke Eli up to find out what he wanted. Eli responded that he had not called, and he sent the boy back to bed. After a while Samuel heard his name called again, but once more Eli told the boy that it was not him. When it happened a third time, Eli knew that it was God calling to Samuel, and he said to the boy, "Go to sleep, and if you are called, reply, 'Speak, LORD, for your servant is listening.'"

The first thing to notice about this story is that everybody expected God to speak to the old priest, but God spoke to the young boy instead. It is important that you be receptive in your youth to the voice of God and not think that God will only speak to you "later." God is speaking to you now—in the Scriptures, in Jesus Christ, in the Church, and in your life experiences.

The other point of the story is that, in order to hear God speaking to us, we must be listening. Samuel would never have received God's message if he had not listened, and the same thing applies to us. Our lives are busy, with plenty of noise. We need to learn how to cut through all the noise and listen to God speaking to us.

Resources

Bibles

The following editions of the Bible contain the full set of biblical books recognized by the Catholic Church, along with a great deal of useful explanatory material:

➤ The Catholic Youth Bible (Saint Mary's Press), which can be ordered with either the New American Bible or the New Revised Standard Version

➤ Student Bible for Catholics (Thomas Nelson Publishers), which uses the text of the New American Bible

➤ The Catholic Study Bible (Oxford University Press), which uses the text of the New American Bible

➤ The Catholic Bible: Personal Study Edition (Oxford University Press), which also uses the text of the New American Bible

Additional Sources

➤ Kirtlink, Sara. "Receive the Holy Spirit," *Youth Update,* Cincinnati, Ohio: St. Anthony Messenger Press, June 1993.

➤ Kurz, William S. and Robert J. Karris, *Acts of the Apostles,* Collegeville, Minn.: Liturgical Press, 1985.

➤ McNamer, Elizabeth. "Travels With Luke: From Jerusalem to Rome," *Scripture from Scratch,* Cincinnati, Ohio: St. Anthony Messenger Press, January 2004.

Available in the Six Weeks with the Bible for Catholic Teens series

Theme: God Reveals Himself to Us

Genesis 1–11: God Makes a Start
ISBN-13: 978-0-8294-2050-0; ISBN-10: 0-8294-2050-9

Exodus: God to the Rescue
ISBN-13: 978-0-8294-2051-7; ISBN-10: 0-8294-2051-7

Luke: The Good News of God's Mercy
ISBN-13: 978-0-8294-2052-4; ISBN-10: 0-8294-2052-5

Revelation: God's Gift of Hope
ISBN-13: 978-0-8294-2049-4; ISBN-10: 0-8294-2049-5

Theme: Jesus and His Disciples

Mark: Getting to Know Jesus
ISBN-13: 978-0-8294-2082-1; ISBN-10: 0-8294-2082-7

John 1–10: I Am the Bread of Life
ISBN-13: 978-0-8294-2083-8; ISBN-10: 0-8294-2083-5

John 11–21: My Peace I Give You
ISBN-13: 978-0-8294-2084-5; ISBN-10: 0-8294-2084-3

Acts: The Good News of the Holy Spirit
ISBN-13: 978-0-8294-2085-2; ISBN-10: 0-8294-2085-1

For more information or to order, please call 800-621-1008. Volume discounts available.